THE REASONABLE ADVENTURER

ROY HEATH

The Reasonable Adventurer

A Study of the Development of Thirty-Six Undergraduates at Princeton

———

Foreword by David Riesman

University of Pittsburgh Press

Copyright 1964 by University of Pittsburgh Press
Library of Congress Catalog Card Number 64-12487
ISBN 0-8229-5071-5
6th Printing 1972

Printed in the United States of America

Dedication

This book is affectionately dedicated to
the thirty-six men of the Class of 1954 Advisee Project
at Princeton University

Jefferson Alison III	Grant Irey, Jr.
Nicholas Angell	Harold E. Jackson, Jr.
Guthrie Baker	Preston B. Kavanagh, Jr.
Henry F. Baldwin	Sidney L. Kleeman
John M. Bergland III	Wesley W. Marple, Jr.
Edward H. Breisacher, Jr.	Charles W. Millard III
John G. Campbell	Ronald B. Miller
Dan L. Chestnut	Sydnor B. Penick III
Norman Fox	Shepherd Roberts
Mark A. Fuller, Jr.	Paul Sarbanes
Robert J. Gaines	John H. Slater
David I. Granger	Claude A. Smith
James H. Greenwald	Edward S. Stimpson
Paul F. Griffin	Charles L. Terry III
Dean W. Harrison	Peter Van Osdol
Brandon Hart	Henry R. Whitehouse
Robert I. Hauben	Alon P. Winnie

In Memoriam
John W. Doberstein   John K. Ewing IV

Foreword

Roy Heath, a clinical psychologist, picked a sample of thirty-six entering freshmen in the Princeton class of 1954 whom he would see as their preceptor or academic counselor, once a week throughout their years at the college. He matched this group, chosen to represent various dichotomies within the University such as public *vs.* private high school, Princeton family *vs.* non-Princeton family, and scholarship aid *vs.* family backing, against an apparently similar group who were to be the controls, not seen by Dr. Heath, and followed only at a distance. One story in this book concerns some of the presumptive effects of Dr. Heath's plainly benign intervention in the lives of the experimental group. The latter did better by Princeton definition in almost every way: they won both more academic and more non-academic honors, including class office, debating, running the campus radio station and so on.[1] So far, the Princeton "experiment" resembles ever so many others which benefit (or, some would say, suffer)

1. Dr. Heath is inclined to think that students who run the student government and edit the daily paper exploit themselves to the University's benefit and their own developmental disadvantage. I would share this judgment in many instances. But as a sporadic reader of the *Daily Princetonian,* I am not sure it is a poorer curriculum for some of its more enterprising editors than what they might otherwise be finding in or out of their course work: that depends on many other things. I do agree with Dr. Heath and many of his advisees that the writing of a senior honors thesis is the single most educative experience an undergraduate can have, and that the sense of accomplishment that results from a well-completed task can carry over into many other aspects of life and work.

from what has come to be called the "Hawthorne effect," namely, the observation first made at the Hawthorne Plant of the Western Electric Company that if one studies human beings they tend to blossom from the mere fact that somebody listens, somebody pays attention. Dr. Heath was a good listener—indeed, judging from interview transcripts appended to the book, almost too good, for in these at any rate, he seems hardly to have challenged the students in any dialectical way but to have been accepting and non-threatening throughout.

Moreover, Dr. Heath brought together groups of eight or nine of his advisees for social evenings where he could observe the interaction of students with each other as well as with him, and this apparently served to create a certain morale as well as friendly contacts among his advisees which, in the often impersonal and frightening atmosphere created for many high school students who come away from home for the first time to attend Princeton, gave a place of anchorage and even of solidarity which may have had a cumulative effect on their careers in college.

In considering this aspect of Dr. Heath's work, I believe it important to notice that he was not only a counselor equipped with psychological skills, extramural to the actual academic process, but also a preceptor with specific academic duties, and one who had himself attended Princeton. Very often, the adviser in a large university is someone ancillary to the teaching process who may be tempted to interpret, for example, blockages in work as the result of Oedipal problems—problems that are no doubt present but that may not be the whole story, whereas someone closer to the academic scene may realize the impact of particular course material or competition within a certain class in focusing or concretizing tensions that may have their roots in the family triangle. On the other hand, an adviser who knows only the curricular situation and brings only his brand of common sense to cope with students' psychological conflicts may be too innocent or too rationalistic in dealing with students. Dr. Heath's blend of the academic and the interpersonal may well have been unusually comforting and clarifying to students.

Not only did many of the advisees win honors by Princeton definitions, but also in the course of the four years perhaps a third of the group moved markedly in the direction of the kind of openness and spontaneity combined with good judgment which Dr. Heath came to call the attitude of the Reasonable Adventurer. Although Tolstoi in a famous sentence maintained that all happy families are alike, these Reasonable Adventurers became less alike: they were experimental but their openness to experience differentiated them both from each other and from the three groupings of less autonomous students whom Dr. Heath terms the Non-committers, Hustlers, and Plungers.

These three constellations first revealed themselves in the styles of response in interviews Dr. Heath had with his advisees. There were some very polite and cautious ones who, when asked, "How are things going," would answer, "Fine, sir," and wait for the next lead. This turned out also to be their response to life: they held back and waited for leads—and knew so little about themselves that they really believed things were fine. The second group came to the interview with a prepared statement as if it were an exam, and at first hearing the statement appeared complete as well as cogent and relevant. Only later did other events and attitudes leak out. These young men turned out to be the Hustlers, "mesomorphic" types, activist, competitive, tough, and assertive. (I was going to say self-assertive but it becomes clear in Dr. Heath's discussion that the Hustler is at war with himself, concealing his ambivalence by activity in an almost muscular way.[2])

The third type of interviewee Dr. Heath called "the roller boys"; these would shift from one topic to another in terms of their own free associations, and would respond or not depending on their mood and that day's tempo. In their general style, these were the Plungers, attuned to their inner feelings so completely that their situational behavior was often random and disconnected. Unlike the Non-committers and Hustlers, both of whom were intolerant of ambiguity, the Plungers gloried in it and had a high tolerance for anxiety. For them, the problem of identity was serious and they suffered the problems of Pirandello's characters. Several majored in philosophy (the Hustlers avoided the humanities) and those in the advisee group interested in the theater were in the Plunger group.

The fourth kind of reaction in the interview was that of the reflective person: six or seven students capable of what Charles Morris terms detached-attachment, able to play with ideas while remaining related to the other person. These young men could both learn and teach and were the Reasonable Adventurers, not so rash as the Plungers nor so inhibited as the Non-committers nor yet so driven as the Hustlers.

2. In Charles Morris's *Paths of Life* (New York, 1942), an interesting attempt is made to relate Sheldon's somatotypes to philosophical and psychological outlook. I believe that one difficulty in this sort of use of the concept of temperament is that we do not know the extent to which our culture helps cue people of a certain body shape to behave in certain ways, encouraging the mesomorph, for example, to a psychological muscularity and activism, while regarding the ectomorph as lacking in the proper shape. Dr. Heath employs the concept of temperament, and while I am sure that these matters of build and physiology do tilt individuals in one or another direction psychologically, I think it is confusing not to recognize the assist our culture provides for such tilting.

In general, Dr. Heath's discussion of personality dynamics and his use of such terms as "ego-psychology" seem to me unilluminating, but that is probably a matter of allergy and personal taste.

Students both of education and of American culture may find these types suggestive, as I have. One might indeed some day be able to classify social strata, whole countries, and colleges in terms of the hegemony of one or another of these types or of various symbiotic relationships among them.[3] Dr. Heath is inclined to think that life in a residential college such as Princeton encourages the development of Reasonable Adventurers, one of whose characteristics is the capacity for close friendships with same-sex peers. Yet the evidence from the interviews presented in Appendix A, so it seems to me, puts Princeton and perhaps all elite colleges in a rather dim light. These students, even as seniors, talked in clichés and seemed to lack at-homeness with ideas. They reminded me all too strongly of a Princeton senior in the class of 1955 whose response to the question as to what life would be like for him in fifteen years I have quoted elsewhere:

> Life will not be a burden for me at thirty-five because I will be securely anchored in my family. My main emotional ties will center in my wife and family—remember, I hope for five children. Yes, I can describe my wife [a hypothetical person]. She will be the Grace Kelly, camel's-hair-coat type. Feet on the ground, and not an empty shell or a fake. Although an Ivy League type, she will also be centered in the home, a housewife. Perhaps at forty-five, with the children grown up, she will go in for hospital work and so on. . . . And improving herself culturally and thus bringing a deeper sense of culture into our home will be one of her main interests in fifteen years. . . . In fifteen years I look forward to a constant level of happiness.[4]

3. Dr. Heath was able to observe such symbioses in the group sessions he arranged and he presents an amusing sequence illustrative of the behavior of the three non-autonomous types when confronted with each other.

4. "The Found Generation," *The American Scholar*, XXV, No. 4 (Autumn 1956), p. 432; reprinted in *Abundance for What? and Other Essays* (New York, 1964).

Of course, there are other sorts of students at Princeton, but it seems to this writer that the fact that it is a stag school, with girls a sometime thing, hampers the intellectual and moral development of the students; and perhaps its idyllic location leads to a certain encapsulation also, despite the increasingly able student body and a scholarly faculty more devoted to undergraduate education than is evident in most other great universities. Or, to put all this in a different way, I am inclined from the material presented in this book to think that Dr. Heath applied the label of "Reasonable Adventurer" more generously to his advisees than an outsider, knowing the material only vicariously, might be inclined to do. One could argue that this generosity had self-confirming effects and helped evoke in the students the qualities dimly latent in them. In Dr. Heath's presence and with his encouragement, the Non-committer might become less anxious, the Hustler less Philistine, the Plunger less alienated. In fact, one of the best comments Dr. Heath makes is that each of these types, if he is to move toward the position of the Reasonable Adventurer, requires different educational experiences, just as in the interview he needs to be responded to in a different way. The Hustler, for instance, ordinarily requires a crisis such as a dramatic failure before he is willing to look into himself and stop running; by the same token, continuing success, whether in athletics or in academic work, tends to close off the Hustler from his inner feelings and postpone a reckoning. Without a crisis, the Hustler needs a great deal of affection and acceptance to thaw out; in the presence of Plungers his defenses may be melted.

The Plunger, in contrast, requires understanding from teachers who can see the structure in his surrealist responses and help him find form without being cramped. From this book it would appear that Princeton rewards the creative Plunger who can externalize his inner ferment, but that the latter pays a high price in misunderstanding. In other colleges—there are only a few, perhaps—where there are more Plungers and where they are the visible stars, life may be made hard for the orderly ones, not similarly egocentric or eccentric, who cannot so readily dramatize their inner lives or so easily antagonize the adult squares.[5]

The majority of the advisees, as Dr. Heath points out in Chapter 6, had come to Princeton with very little interest in academic work which they felt as something imposed from outside by school discipline or by what one is supposed to do at age seventeen. Most of them would not have thought of themselves as intellectuals, a type they consigned to Harvard. But by senior year their attitudes had changed. As already stated, many had profited greatly from writing a thesis. Their affects had in some cases become hitched to particular disciplines and topics in that mysterious way in which a college senior will say of himself, "I'm a biophysicist with an interest in the morphology of the cell," or, "I'm in eighteenth-century literature."

5. It is not necessarily the Plungers who will present themselves as "problems" to the college authorities. When I read Dr. Heath's description of the Non-committers, I recalled a conference seven years ago of the American Council on Education where a number of college presidents were discussing the panty raids and more serious riots that had plagued their campuses, often causing serious damage to people and property. What puzzled the presidents was that the students engaged in these riots were so mild when seen as individuals and that many riots seemed to have no ringleaders, no hoodlum elements, and yet had ended in wild rampages in which people could have been maimed and even killed. The Non-committer, once he feels that permission is given, lacks the experience of his own anger and can become quite ferocious. I am inclined to think that the politics of the Non-committer on the American scene can be equally damaging, for it is an ethnocentric type, convinced of its own rightness, cautious enough to do what everyone else is doing—"above politics" in the way, for instance, President Eisenhower thought himself to be above politics.

In the statements quoted by Dr. Heath, many declare that they have become more interested in books and in ideas. Yet, I am left wondering whether the Princeton faculty would be satisfied with these remarks as indicative that the University had really added something to the endowments with which these students came. In fact, some of these quotations sound like the complacent travesties of sophistication in *The Unsilent Generation*,[6] a collection of interviews with Princeton students of a few years ago. I could interpret these materials less badly if I had a better sense of the regional and ethnic backgrounds of these students, and Dr. Heath (perhaps to avoid identifying individuals) does not give us this. Hence, the trajectory of these students remains opaque, and so does the relation of their temperaments to what may have been approved or disapproved in the upper-middle class of a small Southern town or at the Bronx High School of Science or Philadelphia's Main Line or all the other enclaves from which young men come to Princeton.

In my criticisms of the interviews, I do not think I am speaking merely for a particular type of sophistication which strenuously avoids clichés or corn. The unguardedness of many of these Princeton students is, if one must choose, preferable to the near-paranoid guardedness one can find in the avant garde. And it would not deny the value of Dr. Heath's model if it could be shown by reanalysis that none of the thirty-six by stricter standards could be called "Reasonable Adventurers." We know there *are* such adventurers and that it is one of the aims of a university to help its students move in that direction. It is clarifying to have shown with illustrative case material some of the varieties and sub-varieties to be found

6. Otto Butz, ed., *The Unsilent Generation: An Anonymous Symposium in Which Eleven College Seniors Look at Themselves and Their World* (New York, 1958).

in our colleges, and how differently these react to what is apparently the same curricular fare. If one were as despairing about higher education as this writer sometimes becomes, one could give thanks that none of these students apparently became less reasonable and less adventurous at Princeton; if anything, the contrary. Some students were shaken loose from their bigotries, and one or two Plungers apparently found a frame of understanding, perhaps even an ideology or philosophy, within which to locate their fluid experiences (though no student in the group seems to have undergone a religious conversion). Perhaps by adding Dr. Heath's presence to the other more happenstance encounters with the curriculum and the extracurriculum, the lacunae in the college experience of many of the advisees could be filled in. We do not know, of course, what happened to the others, the over-700 Princeton men who were not in the experimental group. Perhaps some of these took away less than they came with.

I would be pretty sure that Princeton in 1964 is very different from Princeton in 1954—so much so that the sons of Princeton alumni may be among those most badly prepared for the actual Princeton of today. If it is to be judged in any way negatively from the quotations in this book, which would be unfair, it should also be judged sympathetically for its willingness to allow such an experiment as Dr. Heath's. For colleges on the whole have been very backward as compared with industry or the Army in their curiosity about their own inner processes. They are administered by men who have on the whole not been trained for such work, and students are taught by men who have studied their subjects but not the problems of teaching itself or the dilemmas created by the selection and situation of a particular student body. We do not even know if Dr. Heath is right in supposing that growth toward the position of the Reasonable Adventurer requires a residential college with the close ties among students this allows. For one thing, the residential college such as Princeton attracts a student body of whom a sizable proportion are capable of viewing learning as something done "for its own sake," not for the sake of immediate vocational aims, whereas our commuter colleges are attended by students for whom college is the obvious step into the white-collar occupational world. Hence, while I myself am inclined to think that the residential college has the greater impact and the colleges cited by Philip E. Jacob as having "peculiar potency" are residential, it seems to me conceivable that a commuter college, by heroic experimentation, could become almost equally potent.[7] But this would require faculty members willing to spend as much time with students as Dr. Heath spent with his advisees. This would be luxurious education, just as psychoanalysis is a luxurious process in its willingness to spend endless time with individuals who may not be in any way important to the functioning of society. Ours is in some measure an affluent society which should be able to afford such luxuries, if it takes seriously its commitment to nourishing individuality, for this requires exposing students to alternatives beyond their own often all-too-well-defended horizons.

We are well aware of this necessity when we deal with students from deprived cultural backgrounds, for whom college is the first opportunity to transcend a confining milieu. But as our more selective and elite institutions become increasingly demanding and competitive academically, even the more highly endowed and capable students may need for their further development some kind of un-

7. Philip E. Jacob, *Changing Values in College: An Exploratory Study of the Impact of College Teaching* (New York, 1957) ; but cf. also my critique in "The Influence of Student Culture and Faculty Values in the American College," *The Yearbook of Education, 1959* (London, 1960).

contaminated relation to non-parental adults—and when I say "uncontaminated," what I mean is: not distracted either by the grading relationship or by the obligation to become (or to reject becoming) a disciple in the field in which a professor teaches. It is sometimes difficult for a bright and highly motivated student to know whether he is bucking for an "A" or deeply interested in the subject or drawn to a particular instructor. And it is sometimes hard for the instructor to know to what extent his student is seen as "his" student, carrying on his academic mission, reliving his youth, or whatever else. Dr. Heath in his relation to his own students, judging from this volume, put himself into the position of a coach who can respond to students on more levels than their prowess in his discipline. At best, he wanted nothing of them beyond their development as Reasonable Adventurers. And one of the nice things about such adventurers is that, although as I have said they differ from each other, they are capable of nurturing each other along the several roads taken.

David Riesman
Cambridge, Massachusetts
November 1, 1963

Acknowledgments

My gratitude to all the members of the Advisee Project is indicated by my dedication. When I have quoted from student interviews I have done so with the permission of the individuals, and I am especially appreciative of their cooperation. With the exception of the names listed on the dedication page, all names of students are fictitious; for example, the "Bob" who is quoted at length does not exist among the Roberts of the Advisee Project.

In addition I am happy to acknowledge my indebtedness to:

Frederick F. Stephan, director of the Study of Education at Princeton. The idea of a longitudinal study of a small number of students was his. Without his flow of ideas, kindly criticism, and steadfast support the writer would not have been able to bring the Advisee Project to completion. Other colleagues in the Study of Education, Augustus D. Daily, Douglas Bray, Duncan MacRae, Katherine Bell, James Davie, and Paul Hare assisted in the early design of the project. Mrs. Paul Mott carried a heavy load in typing the interview transcripts.

Hadley Cantril, Warren Wittreich, Dean Allen, Irving Alexander, and Silvan Tomkins, colleagues of the writer in the Princeton Psychology Department, for providing criticism and helpful comment in the formulation of the personality model used in this study.

Hermann Muelder, Charles Bumstead, Robert S. Harper, Philip Haring, Paul Shepard, Daniel Kimble,

David Yount, Duane Paluska, Whitton Humphreys, and Robert Peters—all fellow faculty and students at Knox College—for assistance to the writer in his attempt to test the findings of the Advisee Project in a new setting.

Harold W. Dodds, former president of Princeton, for the statements of two of his predecessors—John Witherspoon and Woodrow Wilson.

Frank R. Denton, Charles H. Peake, and Alan C. Rankin, of the University of Pittsburgh, each in his way did much to encourage the completion of this book.

Lela Denman for her assistance in the preparation of the manuscript.

The Carnegie Corporation of New York. Out of their generous grant to Princeton University came the funds to defray the cost of the Advisee Project.

The Edgar J. Kaufmann Charitable Foundation, Pittsburgh, Pennsylvania, for their subvention for the publication of the book.

Table of Contents

List of Illustrations

Introduction

The development of the mind can be broadly construed. So it was in a study of a small number of undergraduates at Princeton. The Advisee Project, as it was known locally, was undertaken in 1950 at a time when Princeton was in the midst of evaluating her effectiveness in the education of young men. To this end a variety of research studies were already in progress. These and the Advisee Project were made possible by a grant from the Carnegie Corporation of New York.

By 1950 the wave of World War II veterans had moved on. We had every reason to believe that the campus was ready to settle back into its traditional pattern. This was a good time, it was thought, to observe the diverse fortunes of the incoming class throughout the four years of their college life. As a sample [1] of that incoming class thirty-six liberal arts candidates found themselves the principal subjects of an evaluation study and assigned to a rather special kind of faculty adviser. I came to this assignment from a background of teaching and practice in clinical psychology. As their adviser I would be talking with these men regularly as individuals and as participants in small group discussions. What made the adviser-advisee relationship special was my freedom to devote full time to this study, for their first two years at least. I was to concentrate upon a single task, viz., to observe, ponder, and, if possible, formulate the impact of a particular university upon

[1]. See Appendix B for notes on the selection of the sample.

the lives of these men. Impacts, of course, work both ways.

This then was the design of the Advisee Project, small in number but comprehensive in its concern for the total experience of each man. From this perspective I hoped to discern some answers to a central question: Did these men grow? What follows is a report of this study to those interested in the growth and development of students in higher education.

The findings of any study of this nature must be interpreted in terms of the setting. One might say that nearly every college and university, for better or for worse, finds itself endowed with a particular image and highly resistant to any administrative attempts to change it. Princeton, in this respect, is no exception. The sub-culture the new student encounters at Princeton is endowed with the values and mores of the homes, neighborhoods, schools, and summer camps of those drawn in years past to the image of Princeton. The composition of the student body since World War II has moved noticeably from being drawn so exclusively from the upper middle class. Yet a rereading of F. Scott Fitzgerald's *This Side of Paradise* is still relevant.

In educational objectives Princeton is unashamedly devoted to the liberal arts. At the undergraduate level, acquisition of knowledge is primarily a means to an end. The end is the person and his development toward a love of learning for its own sake. Through exposure to the humanities, the social and natural sciences, something deep and enobling is supposed to happen to the student, his sensibilities, critical thinking, and awareness of broad perspectives. An early president of Princeton, John Witherspoon, stated the developmental objective well when he said, "The end of a liberal education is to set all human powers in motion."

With Princeton's setting and potential thrust in mind

let us turn to the project itself. One month before my thirty-six advisees arrived on campus I traveled to each one's home to engage him in a lengthy discussion of his life to date and his expectations of college. Incoming freshmen are the most willing and vital creatures on earth. I found my new charges no exception. They were delightfully expectant.

Chapter 1

The Early Impressions and Search for a Framework

The academic year was underway, one week following another all too quickly. The men were coming in regularly for their conferences and, as a rule, promptly. To me they were amazingly free in talking about their experiences. What perhaps is more significant, some were beginning to reflect upon what these experiences were meaning to them.

During the first two or three months my perception of the Advisee group was undergoing what might be characterized as a process of differentiation. Each person was standing out in clearer relief. Behind all this, I was growing uncomfortable for the lack of any conscious framework of growth and development. Fortunately, no one was pressing me on this point. Benefitted, perhaps, by the pause of Christmas vacation, two patterns began to emerge. Regarding the first pattern, I found myself grouping my advisees into four modes of behavior in the interview itself, four ways of relating to me in this context.

Modes of Behavior in the Interview

1. *The one or two worders.* These men used more than one or two words, of course, but the label was derived from the fact that their replies to my questions were generally brief. For example, many of the interviews opened in a non-directive fashion with, "How are things going?" To this they would often reply, "Fine, sir" and await politely

my next question. I was searching for clues regarding their thoughts and feelings. They, in turn, were waiting for some cue from me regarding what I wanted them to talk about. Either no thoughts at the moment were pressing for expression, or if there were some emergent ideas, the students preferred to assume a cautious stance and let me develop the course of the conversation. Occasionally they would begin with a comment on the weather or some passing event on the campus for which they bore no personal responsibility. I did not interpret this as negativism. Their demeanor was generally bland and friendly, remarkably free of hostility.

When I would wait them out with a long pause, a slight rise in tension would be noticeable. But the increase in tension seemed to inhibit them further. In short, I had to carry the ball.

2. *The prepared-statement men.* This group apparently took very seriously their project duty of reporting their experiences. More than others, they seemed to anticipate my questions and arrive for their sessions prepared to give a well-organized account of their activities to date. They talked in paragraphs.

The men in this category had a flare for promptness. They were visibly annoyed should the preceding session with another student run over and into their allotted time. Their conference with me was probably only one of a series of commitments in a tightly planned schedule.

For the prepared-statement men a pause in the interview sequence was tension inducing. When a pause did threaten to be uncomfortable, the student usually continued with an elaboration of a previously stated idea. In contrast to the one or two worders, he would in this way fill in the temporal gaps as they arose.

At first I received these relevant and well-thought-out statements with due satisfaction. Here I was being presented with complete and coherent notes on the life of a particular student. But were they complete? Months, sometimes years later, the student himself would in retrospect bring up episodes, thoughts, and feelings which had not been entered in the earlier record. Such deletions, consciously done or not, were usually understandable. I soon learned to accept the statements for what they were: the picture of himself that he wanted me (and probably himself as well) to have on that particular day. I tried not to press or probe. We would be in touch for several years to come.

3. *The roller boys.* An interview with a roller boy is quite an experience. He rolls from one subject to another without apparent connection. A connection usually does exist but one that is personal in nature and not shared by others. At times the shift from one thought to another is dramatically disjunctive. I recall a freshman-year interview with a roller boy. He was talking about one of his academic courses. Suddenly, without even a change in tempo, he uttered, "Gee, those shoes are neat!" When I interjected, "What was that about *shoes?*" he was somewhat taken back but grinned. "Oh, I went down to the gym this morning. They issued us our basketball uniforms. You ought to see those shoes; they're great!" To this day I am convinced that this particular thought was never intended for expression at that point. But such behavior seems consistent with the view that the thoughts and feelings of this group are remarkably close to the surface. A reading of one of their interview transcripts presents at times a verbal sequence very close to free association. What it lacks in coherence, however, it makes up for in spontaneity, direct expression of ideas, and feeling.

Another but related aspect of the roller-boy interview is the rise and fall of inflection and tempo. The student may begin quietly and with little feeling, later to crescendo to an emphatic tone as if an internal spring of ideas had been suddenly tapped to bring forth a whole new stream of thought.

Once the interviewer does get his chance to break into the conversation the student will patiently wait until the other party is nearly through, and then resume from where he was interrupted. Some, however, are not even this patient.

4. *The reflective persons.* This was the smallest group of all, totaling not more than six or seven students. The term reflective was given because these men showed a greater capacity than others to reflect upon what they were saying. They would make a statement, toy with it in their mind, and finally reconstruct where necessary. Occasionally they would pose a question and then proceed to answer their own question.

The students in the reflective group were also good listeners, with an interest in sharing ideas. Sometimes the conversation would approach a dialogue in the classical sense. Time seemed to pass unnoticed.

As to content of the interview, it tended to move away from personal reference and toward philosophical issues. Somehow these men seemed to have thought more deeply. There was a freshness to their approach to life. Needless to say, these interviews were for me enjoyable occasions, enriching experiences.

Not everyone in the project fell neatly into one of the four modes of behavior in the interview. Some fitted into intermediate positions from the very beginning. Nor was it anticipated that each advisee would retain the classification of interview behavior initially assigned to him.

Satisfaction and Well-being

Another pattern emerged about the same time that I was drawing distinctions in interview behavior. This second pattern was derived from an inquiry into the realm of satisfaction. What areas of life appeared to be important sources of satisfaction for the thirty-six students? There were obvious differences among the men in the amount of deep satisfaction they were experiencing in college. Some evidenced a zest for life, a sense of well being, and an interest and curiosity about their surroundings. In contrast, others seemed either to be struggling to keep their heads above water or just going along with nothing of significance happening to them, as if life were passing them by.

For those who did find their experiences enlivening and exciting, there seemed to be two principal sources of satisfaction: their academic work and their friendships. Consequently, I attempted to systematize such observations by means of two rating scales, one for satisfaction derived from academic life and the other for satisfaction derived from friendships. Each was a five-point rating scale—a rating of *one* representing low satisfaction; *five,* high satisfaction. Each student was accorded a rating of one to five on each of the two scales: academic and interpersonal satisfaction.[1]

The outcome of the rating process showed that only eight students were rated a *four* or *five* on the satisfaction from academic work scale. It may come as a shock to some that so many of the thirty-six students did not evidence more genuine interest in their studies, but such seemed to be the case. On the satisfaction from friendship scale, twelve students or one-third of the students in the Advisee Project were rated *four* or *five*. At this point an interesting interrelationship became apparent. All eight of the men who were rated *four* or *five* on the first scale were among the twelve who were rated *four* or *five* on the second scale. The intercorrelations became even more exciting

1. See Appendix B for these scales.

when it occurred to me that all seven of the students that closely approximated the "reflective" type of interview behavior were also among the eight and the twelve rated high on the academic work and friendship satisfaction scales respectively.

This was something of a conceptual breakthrough. Here were seven men who gave themselves to their academic work and their friends, and who had demonstrated their capacity to become easily absorbed in serious discussion. Such an "extension of the self" requires what is known technically in the psychology of personality as "integrative ego functioning." What these seven had in common was an integrative personality. It evolved from here that the key concept for the personality model or framework would be ego functioning, with the seven men occupying a relatively high position on one of two basic dimensions of ego functioning. Ego functioning may be defined as the manner in which the self interacts with the world, achieves its satisfaction, and defends itself (or fails to defend itself) from threats to its survival, both external and internal. Behavior is not equivalent to ego functioning. The latter is a construct inferred from the former.

Maintenance of a focus of interest and fascination beyond the self and a demonstrated capacity to relate to another human being on a deep level are important clues to effective ego functioning. Another reflector of good or poor ego functioning is self-perception. Man is presumably one of the few members of the animal kingdom who is an object unto himself. One of the first casualties at the onset of a serious emotional disorder is a clear and realistic image of oneself. Therefore, a third scale was constructed to enable me to rate the students in this important area of personality assessment. It was entitled "Self-understanding and acceptance." [2] Self-objectification might have

2. This scale may be found in Appendix B.

been an alternate title. Maintenance of a self-image is seen as one form of self-projection or extension.

I now possessed a triad of three areas of self-projection or psychological extension, three relationships presumably significant in terms of the degree of integration or emotional maturity of the person: self to self, self to other selves, and self to the world. These three scales merely assisted me in making an overall judgment of a student's intellectual and emotional maturity. (At best such an overall judgment is still, of course, a highly subjective and impressionistic matter. This remained true as well for practically all of the personality judgments of the growth and development of the students in the Advisee Project. Even if such a study were being made today this approach would still generally be necessary, even though some very promising work is being done in the area of student development.)

At this point in the study, then, a *developmental* dimension was taking shape in my mind. The seven men who were rated high on this dimension became objects of special scrutiny to discover what attributes they held in common but did not share with the others, those I had rated lower on the developmental dimension. The outcome of this scrutiny was a cluster of six personality characteristics discussed at length in Chapter Four. These seven students also acquired a name befitting their close approximation to an ideal. I called them Reasonable Adventurers.

A Dimension of Temperament

While I was illuminating those who closely approximated the Reasonable Adventurer, the remaining advisees hovered about in the wings. By February of their freshman year I was beginning to sense that the orderly but assertive prepared-statement men occupied a position *between* the genial but conforming one or two worders on one side and the impulsive but moody roller boys on the other. It was not long before such an ordering became for me conceptually a dimension of *temperament* relating to basic differences, I believe, in the control of impulses. The inhibition of impulses in the one or two worders seem to operate at a deep level, somewhat removed from conscious control. Much of the impulsivity of the prepared-statement men also appeared to be controlled but more consciously so. I believed this group could more easily verbalize their thoughts and feelings should they care to do so. A vigilant censor, however, was usually standing by the helmsman. To change the metaphor, the roller boys more frequently rode their impulses to direct expression, often to the disadvantage of the rider. I came to wonder, and I still wonder, whether this group was temperamentally equipped to invoke the degree of close control over impulses seen in the other two groups.

Accordingly, I placed each man along a scale of temperament from the most extreme one or two worder to the most extreme roller boy.

Thus each member of the Advisee Project was rated subjectively on what became the two basic dimensions of the model or framework. From this beginning I visualized the model as triangular in shape, more precisely as a quarter of a circle. As seen in Figure 1 ("Freshman Year Positions") the developmental dimension ran toward point A while the dimension of temperament was represented by an arc. The lowest arc bounding the bottom of the model ran from point X through a mid-point, Y, to point Z.

Here I encountered a problem of nomenclature. Further observation dictated more comprehensive labels than ones merely descriptive of behavior in the interview. By the end of that first year points A, X, Y, and Z on the model, admittedly abstractions, became in my imagination close to living realities. The X was labeled the

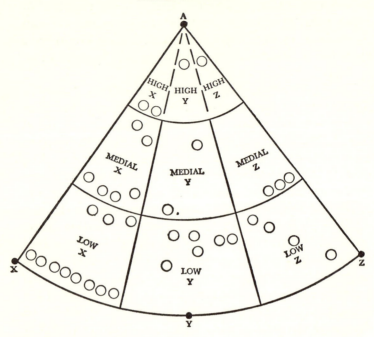

FIGURE I.

Freshman Year Positions

Non-committer because of his general tendency to avoid entangling involvements. The Y, I called the Hustler because of his drive to achieve tangible rewards. The Z was described as the Plunger because of his tendency toward deep involvements, often going off the deep end. Were it not for the obvious existence of intermediate types I would have dropped the rather impersonal four letters of the alphabet. For example, for a person occupying a position in the model halfway between point X and Y, the term Non-committer-Hustler is awkward at best. In such a case the term XY was both more manageable and euphonious.

As a final touch to the model I mapped out seven sections to indicate the approximate positions of the advisees.

As can be seen in Figure 1 each man has a slightly different location in his section according to his relative position on the two major dimensions. Had it been that two or more men were rated precisely the same on the two dimensions (which was not the case), they would have appeared in the model as occupying the same location.

The Beginning of Sophomore Year

Thirty-four of the original thirty-six returned for their second year. Tragically, one advisee had died of blood cancer in the early summer. Another had been dropped for academic deficiencies. As I talked to those settling down to their sophomore year there were more changes apparent than the acquisition of a summer tan and the proverbial proper restraint befitting the year of the eating-club elections known at Princeton as the Bicker. Some low Xs were behaving as medial Xs, a medial Y was acting as if he were a high Y in the A area of the model, and so forth. My freshman-year model position assignments were due for a change, and for most in the direction of the Reasonable Adventurer. None, however, appeared to change on the XYZ arc, the dimension of temperament. I was not about to attribute the developmental changes entirely to summer experiences, even though I could imagine certain of my advisees arguing the point had they known of the existence of the model and their positions on it. No, a more plausible explanation to me was the occurrence of subtle changes during freshman year. It took a summer to break up the rigidity of my perceptions.

We turn next to a description of three prototypes with regard to the dimension of temperament. These are represented on the lowest arc of the model as points X, Y, and Z. The validity of these prototypes rests, for the moment, on the match in your imagination.

Chapter 2

Non-committers, Hustlers, and Plungers

Our Non-committer, the X, is a friendly and generally likeable student. In a group discussion, however, he is usually among the lesser participants. He watches attentively but reveals little of himself. In other situations as well there is a blandness, an under-reactivity, as if his response to inner impulses and external stimuli were somehow muted. In the interview his infrequent references to himself as a person are vague and poorly articulated. Only when his relationship to the interviewer is securely established will he elaborate upon his feelings, particularly in the area of aggression.

The X is named the Non-committer, as we have said, because of his marked tendency to avoid involvements. He apparently views a commitment as a possible entanglement which might reduce his freedom to get out of the way when trouble threatens. When storm clouds do break he'll hold on and hope for the best. In other words, he takes a passive role in a conflict situation.

X's philosophy of "why trouble trouble unless trouble troubles you" is exhibited in many forms during his daily life. For example, in an interview with one of my project members the subject of telephones happened to arise.

"I don't like telephones," he said. "As a matter fact, when I'm alone at home, I rarely answer the phone."

"Why is that?" I asked.

"Oh, I don't know—you never know what might come

up if you do answer the phone. It's probably somebody calling you to ask you to do something, or else they are mad about something. I usually figure everything is O.K. the way things are. So let the damned thing ring!"

X's preference for the *status quo* soon earns him a reputation for being a conservative. His concern to avoid trouble is sometimes naïve because of his indisposition to scout for trouble unless his anxiety is deliberately aroused by an outside force. If only he would turn on his radar, so to speak, he might forestall serious difficulty for himself. X, therefore, more commonly presents a picture of complacency than one of anxiety. For example, during examination time X is apt to make a premature judgment that he has studied sufficiently. Even after writing the examination he might come away with a conviction that he has done at·least passably well, only to be startled and dismayed at the low grade that is subsequently posted. Z, by contrast, tends to leave the examination room convinced that he has done more poorly than he actually has.

X is friendly but his amiability is often geared to keeping the peace. In a secure situation where he feels the acceptance of the group he can be seemingly unrestrained. Watch him closely, however, and you will find he is not taking any calculated risks. Typically, it is the uncalculated acts that get the X into trouble. The two men in the project who were dropped for disciplinary infractions were both Xs. Neither, I am sure, realized their actions might bring such serious consequences. In true X fashion they must have resided in an aura of protective optimism.

I imagine the low X as a deeply embedded personality. His embeddedness, while useful for security and protective purposes, is not viable. In choosing to be in a bed of this sort he is compromising the fulfillment of his basic nature, the expression of his deeper wishes and strivings. For example, he will place a premium on possessing a sense of belonging, of identification with a group even though the group may offer for him little opportunity for self-expression. At least he is safe and there he stays. Somehow he must have a fear of becoming stranded. This reminds me of a certain conference I had with an advisee, whom I'll call Tim, toward the end of his sophomore year. Tim was one of twelve in his class selected to be a chapel deacon. Two other of my advisees were also selected for this honor and all three were, of course, Xs. A chapel deacon at Princeton in addition to having a well-scrubbed look must be genial and friendly. Even though I was familiar with the Princeton chapel services from my own undergraduate days, I asked Tim, "What are the duties of a chapel deacon?"

"We usher or give out programs," Tim said and after a short pause added, "I usually give out programs."

"What about ushering?" I pressed.

"I don't particularly like ushering," Tim went on. "The trouble is that people don't always sit where you want them to sit. Another thing, sometimes when you think you are leading a group up to the front you turn around only to discover that you are way up there by yourself. I'd rather give out programs."

In the neutrality vs. involvement type of crisis why is the X so prone to choose neutrality? True, he wants freedom but freedom for what? This puzzled me for a long time. I finally discovered that some Xs have a secret, a very precious myth about themselves. As protection for the myth they want freedom to bide their time. The great ally of the X is time. One would have to be privy to an X's fantasies in order to realize that the myth is one of invincibility, of high potentiality. He could do a lot of things, the myth says, if he really went all-out. He could make better grades, he could make that team, he could make that girl, etc. Still, day follows upon day and he does not

FIGURE 2.

Freshman Year Model: Positions and College Outcomes

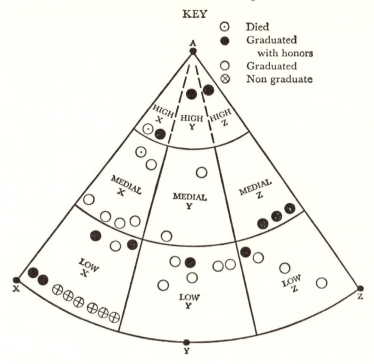

make an honest attempt to do so. But when the right day comes, he says to himself, he shall. The longer he fore-stalls the day, however, the greater the investment in the myth, the more important it becomes to the stability of his self-esteem. To go all-out presents a horrendous risk, namely the discovery that the myth has no basis in fact. Non-Xs seldom realize what high stakes many an X puts on the line when he decides the moment has come *to act.*

The existence of the precious myth provides, perhaps, some clue why Tim and other Xs are so unnerved by an experience of appearing ridiculous. Somehow such exposures connote impotence, and impotence is the very antithesis of invincibility.

Under conditions of lack of response to deeper wishes and strivings, the X's behavior is greatly limited to other persons' requirements of him. He may go along but his total self, his heart, is not in it. He goes along to avoid a fuss. Consequently, his own ideas are tested less frequently. X is a poor learner basically because he has less self-willed experience. In the Advisee Project the scholastic grade averages of those occupying the X segment of the model were consistently lower than their College Boards

FIGURE 3.

College Board Aptitude Scores and Freshman Model Positions
(*Average of SAT V & M*)

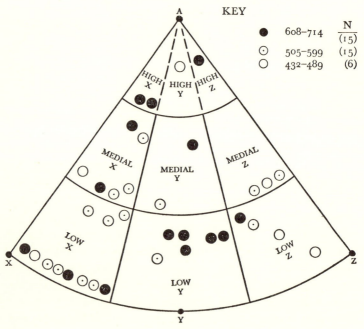

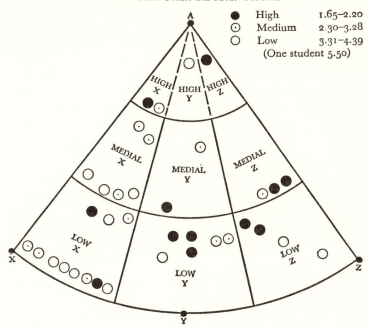

FIGURE 4.

Freshman Year: Grades and Model Positions

●	High	1.65–2.20
⊙	Medium	2.30–3.28
○	Low	3.31–4.39
	(One student 5.50)	

aptitude scores would predict for freshman year. The three students in the project who were dropped for academic failure were Xs. Note Figures 2 ("Freshman Outcomes"), 3 ("Aptitude Scores"), and 4 ("Freshman Grades").

X cannot be described in terms of a single pattern of outward appearance. Xs vary from some who consistently appear cautious and attentive, to others who appear bland, carefree, and deceivingly innocent. Underneath, however, they are much the same. They are all neutralists.

Almost instinctively one comes to handle Xs with care. Theirs is a personality that is easily overwhelmed by high pressure or undue probing. Xs present a serious challenge to our institutions of higher learning. Not the least reason is that there are so many of them.

The Hustler

Y is characteristically a hustler. He thrives on activity but it is purposeful activity. He seems to possess an inordinate need for achievement, for concrete success. In contrast to X, the Y is a fighter, dealing with conflicts aggressively. He scans each new situation for opportunities to demonstrate his worth and superiority over others. He is a great competitor. In his relation with others he is often aggressive and insensitive to their feelings. This is unfortunate for he possesses a strong desire to be received favorably and affectionately.

Y is impatient with the *status quo*. He must keep moving beyond his present level. Wasting time is for him a cardinal sin, a lost opportunity. When there is a lapse in activity he always seems to be raising the question, "What can be done now?" He feels uneasy without some definite plan of action, action that bears promise of paying off in concrete outcomes. He rarely gambles unless he has carefully calculated that the odds are definitely in his favor.

In interviews Y is prone to overintellectualize his motives and idealize his interpersonal relationships, particularly those concerning his family. He is apt to sidestep inquiry regarding deeper feelings, and prefers discussing the personal difficulties of others to those of his own. In discussion groups he can be counted upon to participate early and actively. In that setting, he likes to raise "important questions," demand the "facts," and see that the discussion "gets some place." Also, he is not inclined to hold himself back so that others can speak, a trait that fails to endear him to others in the group. Among those who linger after class to "discuss a point" with the instructor,

FIGURE 5.

Upperclass Majors and Freshman Model Positions

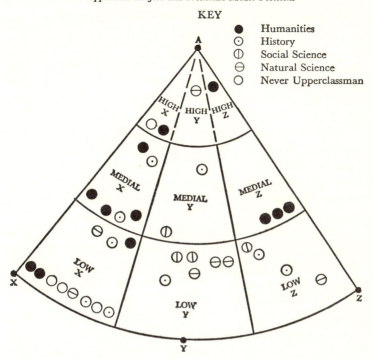

there you will find the Y. Incidentally, he rarely cuts classes or lectures. In the taking of an examination, he is among the last to turn in his paper. In his course selections he characteristically plans far ahead, each course perceived as a building block to reach a particular vocational objective. While he is often a hard working student with a capacity to maintain regular and long study hours, he loses out with his lack of inner reflection and originality.

Y likes to think of himself as being objective, realistic, and above sentimentality. In his philosophical outlook, Y is a "hard guy"; life is a battle. People must look out for themselves, must solve their own problems. He prefers courses that emphasize logic and factual material over courses that require subjective judgment and aesthetic appreciation. As can be seen from Figure 5 ("Upperclass Major") twelve of the project members majored in one or another of the humanities, such as literature, art, philosophy, or religion. It will be noted that *not one* of the nine students classified near the Y point in the model selected a major in the humanities area. They selected either the social or natural sciences. Medicine, law, or government careers seem to attract this type of student.

The Y is a study in antithesis. He makes a good initial impression as a potential student. One soon discovers, however, that he is dealing with a personality that is at war with itself. He is a strong-willed man coupled with equally strong inhibitions and control over his deeper impulses. He rarely allows his feelings direct expression. In short Y distrusts and rejects his inner-self; much of his overt behavior is seen as a counter offensive to nullify the alien instinctual drives, either aggressive or sexual in nature. It is a close battle fought out in the peripheries of consciousness. Attaining success or doing "good" becomes an imperative to offset the "weakness" or "evil" that he suspects is within. Many of Y's conscious goals and values are the antithesis, therefore, of his basic strivings.

This theory would account for many of the puzzling features of Y's behavior. Whenever possible he avoids introspection and keeps his attention instead on his immediate surroundings, on the "here and now." He dreads being left alone presumably because his inner thoughts and feelings make uneasy companions. Even though his interpersonal relationships are superficial, he usually prefers them to no social activity at all. His lack of warmth and originality would be consistent with the notion of counteractive behavior. Also accounted for would be Y's maintenance of unusually high standards for himself

FIGURE 6.

Body Build (Sheldon Types) and Freshman Model Positions

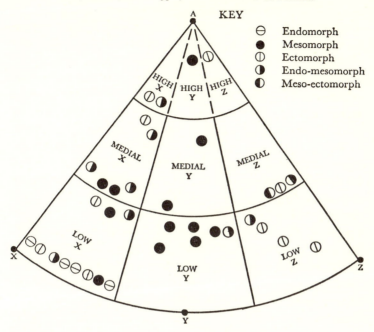

academically, socially, or morally, sometimes far exceeding the expectations of family or associates. He has to keep moving or else lose the battle with himself.

There remains one further aspect of Y that may be of interest. There seems to be a positive relationship between the temperament of the Y and body build. Figure 6 ("Body Build") shows a preponderance of mesomorphs[1] among those occupying the central segment of the per-

---

1. According to Sheldon's classification of body types the endomorph is soft, rounded in body build, and inclined toward accumulation of fatty tissue. The mesomorph is of sturdy structure with a well-developed musculature—the athletic type. The ectomorph is long, slender with poorly muscled extremities. There are intermediate types. See W. H. Sheldon, *The Varieties of Temperament* (New York, 1942).

sonality model. In fact most of the Ys I have come to know seem to be of this muscular athletic type of constitution, an observation, of course, that may be colored by an unconscious bias.

Many Ys come to college well recommended, with high grades and a long list of extracurricular activities. Their transition to college is difficult but the difficulties they encounter may prove to be their salvation, as we shall note in Chapter Six.

The Plunger

The Z is unusual. He is also the least common of the varieties along the dimension of temperament. In contrast to X and Y, the Z has periods when he follows directly the impulse of the moment. His actions are guided by internal criteria. Often with total disregard for propriety, he plunges right ahead. Consequently, he frequently gets himself overextended. In contrast to X, who maintains a remarkable stability of mood, Z is known for his variability of mood. Today he might feel on top of the world, ready to commit himself to anyone or anything that looks interesting or exciting. Tomorrow might find him bitter, sad, alone. His moods ebb and flow as the tides but not as predictably. Whether high or low, he seems at the utter mercy of his feelings. He responds as strongly to guilt as he does to his urges. He lacks the emotional shock absorbers of X.

X is an under-reactor, Y counteracts his feelings, but Z is an over-reactor.[2] He works and loves in spurts. This puzzles both his teachers and his lovers. He may beg permission to go ahead on a project (probably a project he has already started anyway), only to lose interest later, particularly if hard uninteresting work looms. He is quite

2. The writer is indebted to Dr. Henry Ricciuti formerly of the Educational Testing Service, for suggesting this particular distinction.

aware of his inconsistencies but usually at a loss to account for them.

As to interviews, Z baffles any attempt one makes to maintain an orderly schedule. He much prefers to appear when he is in the mood to talk. When this is arranged, he thwarts any attempt to direct the sequence of subject matter. As he releases his feelings regarding a particular experience he may shift without warning or apparent connection to an entirely different subject. In the long run, however, one obtains a frank and coherent picture of a Z's reactions to his college experiences. On occasion he freely shares with you very personal material. The candor of a Z, however, must be protected. He would resent your not doing so for he has moods when he is not so trusting.

In the small discussion group, Z characteristically appears at first to be aloof, indifferent, or preoccupied with his own thoughts. Ys usually start the ball rolling while Xs sit by attentively with eyes shifting from one speaker to the other. It isn't long, however, before something in the discussion strikes a chord in Z and a channel is thereby opened between him and the group. In this shift of attention to the external world, Z also shifts his posture and eagerly gets into the discussion. He is likely to introduce a novel element in order to inject life into the debate. A few Zs in a discussion group are welcome for their natural capacity to serve as "flow men." Like a good brew they help to disarm the reserve of the other participants.

From my comments on the Z's role in the discussion group, it would be wrong to assume that Z always does well in a social setting. In fact, he often has serious difficulty in communication. Since many of his expressions are direct outcroppings of an active inner-self, they are apt to be highly individualistic, even surrealistic. His thoughts zip from one idea to another without apparent connection (zipping like a Z). Consequently, Z is frequently mis-understood and occasionally viewed as a little odd. He does not adjust easily to fine social protocol. X, by way of contrast, likes protocol and does not appreciate the gaucheness of Z which, incidentally, is often intentional. As we have said, X likes to belong and enjoys doing what is proper. The Z, on the other hand, vacillates from wish-ing to be at least noticed socially to experiencing mystical moments when he is above it all. Socially, then, Z resides on an island. He occasionally yearns to bridge the gap between himself and the mainland, but he insists on doing this on his own terms.

Z has a high tolerance for anxiety. He is an active worrier and readily shares his frustration with roommates and friends whether they are prepared to listen or not. X dispels anxiety by repressing or smoothing over threat-ening elements, and Y by compensating activity. Z, how-ever, is left to live with his troubles and resolves his con-flicts by flinging them one way or another.

The fantasies of the Z are as rich as those of the X. The vital difference is that the Z readily acts out his fantasies and thus brings them to an encounter. Probably in the long run he thus comes to a better appreciation of the realities of life. The Z exposes his instinctual thoughts and feelings. I do not believe, for example, that Zs are any better endowed sexually than are their friends to the left in the model. They are just less private with their lusty thoughts and enjoy thrusting them upon those of more delicate sensibilities.

The more hardened sensibility of the Z reminds me of the Toothbrush Test I administered to the Advisee Proj-ect in their junior year. The Toothbrush Test was one of several test situations I devised to elicit a variety of feel-ings they might have toward other members of the project.

Accordingly, the student was placed in a hypothetical situation where he is at a summer camp and has lost his toothbrush. Conveniently, however, as he is washing up for the night, a whole row of toothbrushes is at hand, each one neatly labeled with the name of an Advisee Project member. The student's task was merely to select three toothbrushes he would be willing to use and in what order of preference. The Xs, by and large, were revolted by the whole idea. One said, "I cannot imagine any circumstance under which I would use a toothbrush other than my own. I just can not do this test." The Y's were less resistive and proceeded to be properly selective. The Zs went along readily, intrigued perhaps by the idea. One Z said, "This isn't a good test for me in terms of what I think you are trying to find out. I would use any of them. It does not make any difference which one. I lost my toothbrush months ago and I've been using my roommates' ever since. I'm lucky I have three roommates." Incidentally, the findings of the Toothbrush Test revealed far from a random distribution of selections. Three students do not know it but they had very popular toothbrushes.

An analysis of Z is more readily articulated. One is obviously dealing with a dilated personality whose instinctual life is close to the surface, yielding direct expression of thought and feeling. The picture is complicated, however, by appearances in due succession of a variety of selves. Z plays a variety of roles each consistent with its momentary relevant self. The theatrically inclined members of the project were Zs. They made good actors presumably because they had already played in life many of the roles they are called upon to perform on the stage.

One can well understand why Z is plagued with the problem of identity. Which self is the real self? With shifting selves come changes in attitude, opinions, and out-look. Sooner or later he raises for himself the question of "intellectual honesty." This condition often produces a compelling search for an integrating philosophy to bring greater coherence into his life. It seemed understandable that the two men in the project majoring in philosophy were Zs in good standing.

The Flipped Z

Unfortunately, I can not leave our Zs without mentioning an uncommon but sad possibility. They sometimes flip. This did not happen to any Z in the Advisee Project but I have seen instances of such cases since. When this hap-pens it is usually someone in the lower far-right corner of the model. Society soon runs out of forgiveness for a person characterized by unabated impulsivity. In a tightly regulated social structure a low Z is chopped down again and again. It would take a hearty soul to sustain such odds. Some Zs capitulate and flip from their characteristic internal to external criteria, from inner to outer direc-tion. The outcome is a lost personality in search of an ego. Our flipped Z may then attach himself to a host, more than likely a strong high Y. He follows his alter ego around like a faithful dog grateful for a home.

The flipped Z is usually a quiet and unobtrusive per-sonality. Because he seems anxious to comply with exter-nal standards of behavior he can easily be confused with the appearance of some Xs. There are significant differ-ences, however, between the X and the flipped Z. The latter retains his awareness of a highly varied and intru-sive inner life which is less surgent in the X. Also, strong attachments to an alter ego would be inimical to an X. Xs are leary of becoming trapped into anything so con-fining.

The predicament of the flipped Z is not hopeless but

that is another story. My major concern in this chapter has been to fix for the reader three major reference points on the XYZ arc represented by the Non-committer, the Hustler, and the Plunger. The next chapter will portray our ideal prototype.

Chapter 3

The Reasonable Adventurer

The principal characteristic of the Reasonable Adventurer is his ability to create his own opportunities for satisfaction. Not that some less effective varieties of personality are uninterested in obtaining satisfying experiences but that they seem unable to do so on a sustained basis. The secret of the Reasonable Adventurer's or A's success in this regard seems to lie in a happy combination of two traits,[1] a flare for change and a world relatedness. He is an adventurer but his adventures make sense. As Sidney Hook says of the mature person, he possesses reasonable expectations. He seems to have his psychological house in sufficient order to release him to attack the problems of everyday life with zest and originality. And he seems to do so with an air of playfulness.

The A is characterized by six attributes: intellectuality, close friendships, independence in value judgments, tolerance of ambiguity, breadth of interests, and sense of humor.

Intellectuality. In the pursuit of a problem A appears to experience an alternation of involvement and detachment. The phase of involvement is an intensive and exciting period characterized by curiosity, a narrowing of attention toward some point of interest. It is while "on the prowl" that the person takes this step toward change,

1. The terms *ability* and *trait* are not used here, as they commonly are used, to imply that these attributes are necessarily permanent.

makes a discovery, suddenly perceives a new relationship. This period of involvement is then followed by a period of detachment, an extensive phase, accompanied by a reduction of tension and a broadening range of perception. During this period of detachment there is greater awareness of the presence of the self. Here A settles back to reflect on the meaning of what was discovered during the involved stage. Meaning presumes the existence of a web of thought, a pattern of ideas to which the "new" element can be related. One imagines that this is the sort of mental operation that takes place in a stance often referred to as the critical attitude. Then, after this process of ramification and clarification in the extensive phase, there is an eagerness to be on the way again.

We see, therefore, in A the combination of two mental attitudes: the curious and the critical. They do not occur simultaneously but in alternation. A at times is a "believer" but at other times he is a "skeptic." The less effective personalities may show tendencies toward one attitude or the other but may not experience the full reach of either.

Close friendships. The discussion of the two mental attitudes represents an attempt to spell out the uniqueness of A's relationship to his academic pursuits. Much of what has been said of his intellectual adventures can also, I believe, be said of another form of adventure, his friendships. Here, too, are phases of involvement and detachment. The onset of a close friendship in college is often marked by the experience of "discovering" another individuality. Such a discovery may come quite unexpectedly to both parties. This episode seems to have the same elements of intensity and excitement that characterized the involved phase of intellectual discoveries. It is a sharing of inner-selves that releases the parties for further thought and reflection in a period of detachment that usually follows. In fact, in some way or other, neither party is quite the same again.

If observation of the thirty-six men is a sufficient guide, common interest is less a basis for close friendships than is popularly believed. Studies, athletics, and other activities do, of course, provide media for bringing certain students together but do not seem to be the real basis for the information and maintenance of a friendship. What is the basis? One factor seems to be similar mode of communication. It often turned out that the two parties in a close friendship came from similar regional or social backgrounds so that they found they talked the same language and perhaps shared the same values even though they did not know each other before college. Common background, still, is a superficial factor compared to what I consider to be the main element in a close friendship: the communication of deep feeling. It is not so important that the two parties have shared the same experience as it is that the feeling associated with their respective experiences was essentially the same. It's the *feeling* that became objectified.

Recognition of shared feeling seems to pave the way for another outcome in the formation of a close friendship. A new perception must emerge. This means a new way of looking at oneself, certain people, or at the world in general. The fact that each has discovered through the other a new perception of high personal significance apparently seals the emotional bond in the relationship between the two individuals.

An important distinction between a close friendship and those peer relationships which have a more clearly sexual basis is that the former is more collateral, a relationship between equals. The latter is apt to reflect greater possessiveness toward each other. In the close friendships I observed in the Advisee Project, an attempt to incorporate one another was as lacking as was jealousy. The more friends the other had, the better. The bounds of individuality were shared but not broken.

The establishment of a close friendship in college, I have found, is a common precursor to an intellectual awakening. Many students have spoken of this. They frequently date an enlivened interest in their academic work from the establishment of a close friendship. Incidentally, this close relationship between intellectual and interpersonal development highlights the importance of providing a residential setting in our colleges and universities that is conducive to friendship formation.

Independence in value judgments. Another feature that is associated with A or the Reasonable Adventurer is his relative independence in the area of values. This aspect was particularly observable in small-group discussion or project "precepts." The right or wrong of a particular decision, the goodness or badness of a certain act was less often resolved by reference to external authority. A is more apt to rest upon the authority of his own experience. Where this is not possible, he commonly suspends judgment and finds himself playing the role of the interrogator in the discussion. As such he can ask good questions.

Differences that arise between A and others are not so much taken as a personal affront. Rather, they provide for him an occasion to reflect upon his own judgment. When a difference in judgment is found with a party whom he holds in high regard an argument is usually pursued with vigor and interest. Once I deliberately assembled seven Reasonable Adventures for an evening's discussion. It was a memorable occasion.

Tolerance of ambiguity. Life has its chaotic moments. Such occasions seem less disturbing to A. There is with him less compulsion to relegate matters into black and white. He has greater tolerance for mere shades of gray. When a basis for making a decision is not at hand he is more willing than the less effective personalities to suspend judgment.

It is tempting to account for A's tolerance for ambiguous situations by reference to his relatively stable self-image. When the self is sufficiently objectified in a realistic fashion a psychological base of operations is provided. A, then, enjoys encounters with the unknown. Because of this, perhaps, he displays less compulsion to reduce all unknowns before one acts. The Reasonable Adventurer, in short, preserves the sanctity of the unexpected.

Breadth of interest. The new, the bizarre, and the strange beckon us all. What separates the Reasonable Adventurer from us is his uncommon interest in the commonplace. Somehow in the ordinary more is seen, more is felt. He may have problems of many sorts but for the Reasonable Adventurer the least likely problem is boredom. Can you imagine, for example, a Pascal, an Emerson, or a Churchill being bored?

There is an eagerness about A to get on with a number of projects that he either has started or has in mind for the future. His pursuit of interests differs from the dilettante's. A's interests, in contrast, are better integrated from a breadth that has been achieved through *depth,* a sustained pursuit of a specific problem. This ability to mobilize and maintain one's efforts for a long pull often pays off by thrusting the inquiry to a level where hitherto alien and unrelated areas become known and seen in some kind of relationship. It is an experience that rewards the student in the long run, one that is usually foreign to those who cram for examinations at the last moment and depend heavily upon rote memory. As a matter of fact a sustained period of study is often the best way to restore a flickering fascination. The Reasonable Adventurer has a deep understanding of many areas of knowledge not necessarily because he is more intelligent but because he has been there.

Sense of humor. Perhaps the most winning trait of A's is his lively but benign sense of humor. It rarely takes the caustic form that one associates with an indirect release of pent-up aggression. Rather, A's sense of humor seems to stem from a fluidity of mind that permits him to shift quickly his point of aspect, his angle of view in each situation with which he is confronted. Also, his reservoir of deeper and better digested experiences enables him to see beyond the stereotyped or common view. Such maneuverability and depth, therefore, greatly enhance the possibility for humor. The Reasonable Adventurer makes good company. He is a lively fellow coupled with a keen sensitivity for the feelings of others.

My favorite historical prototype for the Reasonable Adventurer is Benjamin Franklin. At the time of his early retirement from a prosperous business career, Franklin explained his motives in a letter to his friend Cadwallader Colden: ". . . I am in a fair Way of having no other Tasks than such as I shall like to give my self, and of enjoying what I look upon as a great Happiness, Leisure to read, study, make Experiments, and converse at large with such ingenious and worthy Men as are pleas'd to honour me with their Friendship or Acquaintance, on such Points as may produce something for the common Benefit of Mankind, uninterrupted by the little Cares and Fatigues of Business." [2]

I have tried to picture the Reasonable Adventurer as a fully functioning human being, one who is open to new experiences in a changing world. He is seeking the fulfillment of his individuality from a base of world related-

2. Benjamin Franklin to Cadwallader Colden, Sept. 29, 1748, in Leonard W. Labaree, ed., *The Papers of Benjamin Franklin*, III (New Haven, 1961), p. 318.

ness. While this level of functioning is best calculated to bring deep satisfaction it would be wrong to assume that the Reasonable Adventurer exists in a state of undiluted happiness. His happiness is geared to his sympathies and his compassion is broad. His deep awareness that he lives in a troubled world from which he cannot escape is certainly conducive to sobriety and, at times, anguish. A is no superman. In fact, he may be no more than average in mental endowment. What he has he uses well. For this reason he is more fortunate than others. He knows what it means to be alive.

Chapter 4

Elaboration upon the Model

In dreams begins responsibility
W. B. Yeats

The term Reasonable Adventurer is a dialectic connoting two aspects of the individual. Adventure speaks of the inner-self, the spirit, the instinctive urges, the primary processes. Reasonableness speaks of the outer-self, the intellective, the rational, the ego as it copes with its two worlds, within and without. Only in the well-functioning personality does reality achieve depth, coming about through a gentle interweave of the two worlds perceived as one. When this occurs it is a remarkable transaction. In this optimum stance of the individual, represented by point A in the model, the distinction between an inner- and outer-self becomes academic. The person is functioning as a whole.

But we are not always "functioning as a whole." The inadequate stances in life, the various forms of immaturity are almost certain to appear in any general group. In terms of the model, the varieties of immaturity are represented along the lowest XYZ arc. Although many points on this dimension of temperament might bear description, only the three major reference points are noted in terms of the dialectic:

X is reasonable enough but low on adventuring. Due to an alienated inner-self, he takes his cue from others. He lives by external criteria. But his complaints are few as he is unaware that life could be more rich. X goes along, estranged from his inner reaches, and obviously has some investment in the estrangement.

Y is at war with himself. He uses his rational self to contain a suspected inner-self that threatens to break loose. Only by achieving perfection can he be convinced that he is winning the battle. Y keeps trying but is never quite sure that the "good" is good enough. As a result, upon close inspection, he is neither very reasonable nor very adventurous.

Z is adventurous but unreasonably so. He acts as if he had boundless faith in his inner life and characteristically tries to impose it on the world about him. His cues for action are internal. He trusts his feelings, his intuitions whether or not they make sense to others. Occasionally he wins on a long shot, which spurs him onward to mightier notions. He is then due for a crash which will shake him to the core. But the core of a Z is seemingly indomitable. He soon bobs up to try and try again.

Some Precautions

Ego functioning is not behavior. Ego functioning is a construct, an abstraction derived from a host of behavioral items. Were this a model of behavior then it would follow that movement toward the apex, point A, would mean increased similarity of behavior. All Reasonable Adventurers would act alike. This is not the case in our model of ego functioning. In fact, the further toward point A a person develops, the more finely sketched is his individuality. The stereotyped behavior, however, is more common among those lower in the model.

Placement of a person in the model is, in my opinion, a more subtle and difficult judgment than might first appear to be the case. Sometimes the individual himself is the least capable of making a judgment of where he belongs in the model, particularly where he stands at present. He is apt to see characteristics of several prototypes in himself. One need not be a professional psychologist to make a judgment but the observer should possess at least the experience of sustained and careful observation of the individual for whom he is making the judgment. People have a right to resent the abuses of judgments of others not possessing this qualification. It is a sensitive matter.

The Impulse Tether

David Riesman aptly invoked the metaphor of the *tether* in the dialectic of impulse and control when he described the Advisee Project:

Through interviews . . . [the writer] was able to discern attitudes similar to those . . . [the students] exhibited toward the learning process in general. One group was characteristically non-committal; it lived on a short tether of impulse, capable yet cautious, afraid of being "had" or seeming ridiculous, dutiful but unresponsive. Another group was more active in a strenuous, all-American way, their tether of impulse was longer, but still harnessed to the activities especially valued by the peer culture at Princeton. . . . A third group was far more moody; its impulses were often out of control and were connected only with difficulty to the rhythms of the curriculum or extracurriculum. In the interview situation, members of this group could be extremely responsive, even manic, or very depressed or withdrawn. . . . The goal toward which he tried to move all three groups was a level already attained by a handful he called "the Reasonable Adventurers." These were men in whom the dialetic between impulse and control was neither harsh as in the non-committers, nor wholly erratic as in the third group. The Reasonable Adventurer was willing to take chances and to open himself up to new experience, but he was not desperately *driven* to take chances or avoid them. Nor was he, like members of the second group, active and muscular only within the conventions of Princeton; he was willing to allow his impulses a wider arena and to enlarge his imagination.[1]

Creativity

The Reasonable Adventurer is able, as Riesman suggests, to suspend action for an imaginative interplay or toying

1. David Riesman, "The Quality of a College," *Harvard Alumni Bulletin,* Oct. 22, 1960, p. 118.

of ideas. With this kind of interplay a genuinely creative production is a more likely outcome. The less mature groups seem to lack any sustained basis for creativity. The following schematic sequences are intended to portray the creative process in the A as well as the non-creative process which I infer from the behavior of the X, Y, and Z respectively:

FIGURE 7.

Creative Sequence in the A or Reasonable Adventurer

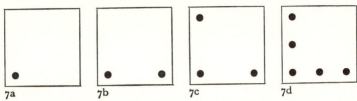

A starts as in Figure 7a with a construct which I will call an "idea." Soon another idea emerges (7b) to be followed by still another (7c). The three ideas are fondled imaginatively and take form (7d). The essential feature in A's sequence is that the ideas as they emerge are sus-

FIGURE 8.

Non-creative Sequence in the X or Non-committer

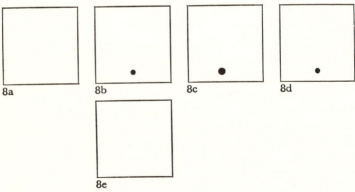

pended for imaginative interplay until some definite form emerges.

X usually starts with an externally directed situation where he must create something, e.g., a poem or theme. He starts then with a blank page (8a). Later, perhaps after a few welcome interruptions, an idea glimmers (8b) and comes into full salience (8c), only to become enfeebled by doubt (8d) and later by rejection (8e).

FIGURE 9.

Non-creative Sequence in the Y or Hustler

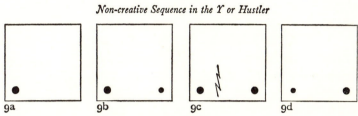

Y finds an idea has entered his mind (9a). As he wonders about this idea another, an antithetical idea, crops up seemingly out of nowhere (9b). The two ideas are examined and considered inimical to each other (9c). Yes, he is sure now, the second idea is much better (9d). Yet the first idea does not quite disappear.

Z experiences a new idea (10a). "It looks great, let's try it," he says and does (10b). But soon the possibilities of the idea are exhausted (10c). He does not have to wait long before a second and very different idea pops in (10d). It too is worth a tumble so away he goes on idea number two (10e). Finally, as it has been a hard day, he rests (10f).

In summary, A suspends action to permit an interplay of ideas which sometimes leads to novel form. X is left with a paucity, an enfeeblement, of ideas because of a very early intervention of control. Y gets caught in an ambiva-

FIGURE 10.

Non-creative Sequence in the Z or Plunger

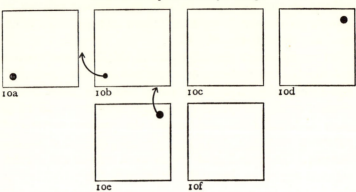

lence that never quite gets resolved. Z dissipates ideas with his disinclination to suspend action.

Intermediate Types

One of the crucial assumptions in the present model or framework of student growth and development is that X, Y, and Z occur as points on a continuum and in that order. Teachers and psychologists are hardly unfamiliar with persons resembling our descriptions of Non-committers, Hustlers, and Plungers, whatever name they might apply to them. To see them aligned on a dimension of temperament may be new.

For reasons of simplicity, I have largely ignored an exposition of intermediate types on the same dimension. For example, there are the XY and YZ who resemble "organization men" and "entrepreneurs" respectively. Even the "left Y" and "right Y" (i.e., to the left and right of the midpoint) can be distinguished easily from each other. The left Y places special emphasis on efficiency and orderly processes, making a good office manager. At the lower levels, he may be compulsively orderly and thereby efficient in only a limited sense. The right Y is less a closed system personality, more enterprising, more willing to risk upheaval in the organization process or system. With his "toughness" there can be a ruthlessness not seen in the left Y.

As we approach the YZ point in the XYZ continuum one sees less emphasis on concrete and tangible "realities" and more willingness to entertain untested ideas. Sometimes a strong emotional investment becomes attached to these untested ideas and we see the familar pattern of paranoid thinking including the externalization of the "enemy." The left Z may try to work within the organizational structure. He lacks, of course, the reliability of the Ys who keep more steadily focused on the here and now, day in and day out. The left Z may make a good idea man, perhaps in some fields a good salesman. His periods of productivity tend to come in spurts, and he should, therefore, pick a job which allows for variation in mood. From my experience with left Zs there seems to exist a tension between the basic narcissism of the Z and a desire to express himself effectively within the structure of an organization. The right Z might align himself with a group only occasionally and then usually by accident. Essentially, the right Z is a "loner" and admittedly not desirous of working over or under anyone. The pity of it is that society seems to have fewer and fewer places for the right Z.

When life for the right Z becomes intolerable he might attach himself to a benign religious symbol. Within the range of Protestant sects the Zs are more attuned to the high church for its well-developed use of symbols and ritual, and also for its relatively high tolerance for varying modes of conduct. Religious conversion is a rich and relatively quiet affair and bears little resemblance to the robust conversion of the Y to a fundamentalist type of religion which offers so much in the way of atonement for "evil" instinctual thoughts and feelings. The fundamentalist churches have more to offer the Ys in the way of demanding strict observances in conduct and concrete opportunities to demonstrate one's worthiness.

Just where Xs belong in this discussion I am not sure. The lower Xs are not genuinely within the reach of any religious appeal. They may go to church and enjoy the sense of belonging to a well-intentioned group. I doubt, however, if any low X is deeply moved by religious symbols.

Inner Dynamics

In a search to make sense out of the many diversities and apparent contradictions of human behavior one finds oneself applying whatever constructs that appear to help. The construct of the ego and its relationship to the inner-self is a construct of ego psychology often referred to as inner dynamics of the personality. Communication is difficult unless one shares the variety of mental pictures, valid or not, that he invokes to imagine the inner workings of a personality. For what they might be worth I would like to share with the reader my own mental pictures of the inner dynamics of the prototypes of X, Y, and Z. The printed page forces a reduction to two dimensions which actually is viewed not only in three dimensions but to a certain degree in motion. To begin, the inner dynamics of the X is illustrated by Figure 11.

I see the self as two concentric spheres, one inside the other. Beyond the wall of the larger sphere is the outer world. The small sphere contains the inner-self or sometimes referred to figuratively as the inner world. The area between the two spheres is the domain of the outer self, the relater of the two worlds. As a low X develops toward point A in the model the wall containing the inner-

FIGURE 11.

Inner Dynamics of the X

self becomes progressively a more porous membrane, so to speak. Also, under conditions of security such as with non-threatening colleagues or friends the X "lets his hair down." The membrane becomes more porous. A few Xs when feeling both safe and excited suddenly become very reactive, almost Z-like, as if the membrane has sprung a leak. These, therefore, might be spoken of as "leaking Xs." Once the excitement subsides the membrane seems to repair itself readily. Most Xs, though, do not leak.

The inner dynamics of the Y are pictured in Figure 12.

FIGURE 12.

Inner Dynamics of the Y

In my image of the Y the wall between the inner and outer selves contains a few openings through which impulses, as denoted by the interior arrow, are continually threatening and pressing for expression and would reach expression in action, were it not for the counteractive effects of the ego to control the flow. The more threatening the impulse, the busier the Y becomes, the counter-actors oscillating back and forth steadily. The counter-actors, the reaction formation, are illustrated in the diagram by the three concentric lines opposing the three gaps in the wall of the inner-self.

The Z, as can be seen in Figure 13, is more completely vulnerable to intrusion from the inner-self, the gaps in the inner-self wall being too wide for effective control. The more one observes Z, however, the more one is inclined to suspect that most Zs have a second level of defense more

FIGURE 13.

Inner Dynamics of the Z

central to the personality. Accessible as they might first appear to be to others, these Zs stop short of going all the way with you, as if reluctant to bare their soul. Some of my associates who are familiar with the model press the point that in the far right Z this area of no access is sizeable.[2]

Quite appropriately, the reader will ask, "What sort of diagram do you have in mind for the Reasonable Adventurer?" I can only reply that all these inner workings dis-

2. The reason some press this point is interesting. Should this actually be true, the far right Z might be joined with the far left X. If these colleagues are correct, then the XYZ continuum comes full circle. I have not yet seen a ZX, but perhaps one does exist. At the present writing we are systematically studying a class of over 1,000 students at the University of Pittsburgh by way of objective measures of the model. If these measures meet certain validity requirements and should one find a ZX or two, the present model will need revision. Naturally, from a scientific point of view a model should satisfactorily contain all known cases. For this reason all uncontained cases should be seized upon for serious study.

THE REASONABLE ADVENTURER

appear as one approaches point A in the model as does the whole distinction between the inner- and outer-self. In a sense so does the self. In terms of my own philosophical outlook, point A is the full life where the dominant emotion is compassion for life, where life is but a game, a game one can choose to play seriously or not. The fact that he is aware that he has a choice is only another way of saying that the self has been transcended. Here the distinction between self and other selves largely evaporates. Most of us become so caught up in the quotidian "inner workings" of society that only in fleeting moments can we get above it all.

The Illustrative Cases in Terms of Inner Dynamics

One of the most effective, though time consuming, instruments for reflecting the inner dynamics of an individual is the Thematic Apperception Test devised by Professor Henry Murray and others at the Harvard Psychological Clinic in 1943. In this test the student is shown in succession a standard series of pictures. He is asked to compose for the examiner a short story about each picture. Three stories are presented here as told for picture card no. 4 of the test series by an X, Y, and Z, respectively. We will name them Henry, Tom, and Dick. Each was a senior at Princeton at the time. In the foreground of this picture are a man and a woman, both young adults. The man is turning away from the woman. In the background on the wall is a calendar-type picture of a partially dressed woman. The writer's comments are in parentheses.

Henry, a High Medial X

HENRY: (He quietly examines the picture for fully two minutes. He sighs as he begins.) These two people are married or engaged or else ready to be married. I think there is some sort of an emotional conflict in this fellow's mind because there is some sort of . . . of mental illusion or mental remembrance in picturing in the mind this woman here whom he might have had relations with and probably did. And he is torn between physical satisfaction here and . . . and true love here. Yet the expression on this woman's face doesn't seem to justify the picture. She doesn't seem as if she is really torn and that's why I don't understand. . . . I . . . I think she is trying to hold him back but she doesn't look very convincing. He definitely wants to go away; I don't think he is even considering her . . . (The student pauses as though finished. Notice how he figuratively hovers over the scene, not inclined to commit himself to a definite theme or definite flow of action. Finally the examiner prods him to go further.)

EXAMINER: What would you say led up to it?

HENRY: I don't know. Apparently . . . apparently he must have met this woman somewhere—in a bar or other place. She might have seduced him or else she might have brought him to her apartment and let him go. Maybe actual . . . actual intercourse wasn't accomplished. . . . But now that he is thinking about her he wants to go back and try again. And he is not even considering her (presumably the woman in the foreground).

Yet she looks as if she knows this and she wants to stop him; and then again, I think she might not want to be so stern or so strict as to completely keep him away, but to let him go and realize his mistake. And then again, I think he will go to her again, this woman he is thinking about, and he will realize how wrong he has been. And I think as soon as he sees this other woman he will realize right on the spot, he won't even consider having any relation with her at all and he will come back to her. And she will feel justified in reacting the way she is now. And that might explain the expression on her face. As it stands, she doesn't look very torn up about. . . . (Note how the stu-

THE REASONABLE ADVENTURER

dent is standing off from the story, interested, but from a distance. Note also the use of qualifiers such as "she looks as if," "I think he will," "she might," and "apparently.")

EXAMINER (pressing for a conclusion): And he will come back ultimately?

HENRY: He will come back ultimately.

EXAMINER: How will things be then?

HENRY: Oh, I guess they will be all right. And I guess he won't entertain any more notions about this woman or any other woman. He looks . . . he looks in a state of blind physical emotion . . . that glaze in his eyes, contorted expression on his face. . . . She looks as if she is the homey type who is right at this moment utilizing her woman's intuition. But eventually I think things will turn out all right. . . . How's that?

EXAMINER: That's fine. About that length. (The examiner finds himself reassuring the student.)

HENRY: God, I couldn't figure out that emotion on her face!

(Even with the prodding from the examiner, this is a far better story than a lower X would have told. The latter would have centered his story on the most salient aspects of the card, ignoring the peripheral and the details. Usually for a low X there is only one single thrust to the story from which he proceeds to complete it with as few complications as possible, as if this main concern is to get the task done and over with. Some low Xs, on the other hand, attempt little more than a mere description or commentary on the picture.)

Tom, a High Medial Y

TOM: (He studies picture for forty-eight seconds, then begins.) This looks like a war poster. Although on second thought, it probably isn't. This picture is confusing. You can consider only these two characters on the right. You can make a perfectly coherent story, but this gal up in the corner with the low-cut dress on throws a monkey wrench into the machinery. There's some writing above it; and there's this picture of this gal looking down. Well, we'll just talk about these two people on the right.

(The ambivalence of the Y is revealed at the outset. Although he is obviously intrigued by the poster girl in the upper left of the picture, he decides to restrict his story to the couple on the right.)

The man is obviously leaving. There is a look of determination in his face and in his eyes particularly. His chin is stuck out like he looks like he's going somewhere. From the intense look on his face—intelligent look, I think—I don't think he's going to go chasing this low-cut dressed gal on his left; he looks like he's going to do some work— he's been called away by his conscience, or some thought of his that he has something to do.

(Sex lingers, however. Note how he counters sex by endowing the hero with determination and intelligence. Rather than chasing the "gal," his main character is "going to do some work," is "called away by his conscience," has "some thought . . . that he has something to do.")

The gal on the right in the white dress looks very much like she's a nurse; at any rate, she's in love with this guy and she doesn't want him to leave and from the look on her face, I don't think they are married. She looks as if she's a little bit overpowered by his determination and although she's not consenting one bit in letting him go, I think she looks like she knows he's going. She is the clean-cut, all-American girl as opposed to this other number on the left, and she looks like she's interested in keeping him home; the lace curtains on the right at the window suggesting domestic tranquility. It is a complete contrast to this frilly dame; the implication is planted there. But on the other hand, the look on his face and the look of respect on her face as she's looking at him, I think intimates that she, the low-cut dressed gal, isn't the reason that this man is leaving. I can't fit her into the picture at all. I mean I can fit her in but I don't think . . . the rest of the picture doesn't seem to suggest that.

(The girl in the foreground becomes projected as the very antithesis of the "frilly dame" on the left. The former is "the clean-cut, all-American girl" in a scene "suggesting domestic tranquility." What a reaction-formation! As anyone familiar with this test knows, this picture is perhaps the least likely to elicit ideas of domestic tranquility.)

As far as the outcome is concerned, it is pretty obvious this guy is leaving; he's going to go and this other girl on the right will stick around. Happy ending. I don't think this low-cut dressed gal belongs in the picture.

(The outer-self triumphs over the alien instinctual life, almost. A lower Y's story would have been more concrete in terms of action and far less explicit than Tom's about the ambivalent thoughts and feelings. To me this illustrates one of the important differences between a medial Y and a low Y. The medial Y is more aware of his unresolved conflicts and is even willing to share a few with those he trusts.)

Dick, a High Medial Z

DICK: (He pauses for seventeen seconds only, then moves in directly.) This is a picture of a guy in some kind of brothel—a whorehouse of some kind. This prostitute here, on the right, is in love with this guy—one of those Ernest Hemingway deals.

Another prostitute comes in. She can be seen in the mirror, in the background. (He turns to examiner.) You can see her in the mirror. The guy is turning to look at her. You see, he loves her—that is, he loves the other one

—not the one who loves him. That one is all over him. She's holding on to him.

But he likes the other one. He has a kind of love for the other one. Not platonic, mind you, but physical. She's coming into the room . . . sees these two in the room. She sees the first one trying to seduce the guy. He, at one time, liked her . . . but not any more.

The other one is peeling off her clothes. She knows she has him on her little finger, and she's enjoying it. She knows that he's hot on her. She's down to her slip now.

He has seen her. He's kinda biting his lips; he wants her. She has a sort of shrewd look in her eye. She doesn't like the other girl, so she's glad to seduce this guy she loves.

The outcome is that he'll try to get at her, but that this prostitute who loves him is going to try to interfere. He's gonna throw her against the wall . . . he is going to hop over to the other one. He's gonna seduce her. He's going to ask her to shack.

The other one—the frustrated lover—will be angry. He doesn't care. He's dominated by animal instinct.

(Dick cleverly incorporates the poster gal into an actual presence in the room. Note his ready use of robust, strong language. There is direct and progressive action throughout: "He's hot on her," "He's kinda biting his lips," "He's gonna throw her against the wall." The student obviously has an easy acceptance of instinctual impulses. Furthermore, I suspect the Z here rather enjoyed the impact of the story upon the examiner. A high Z story. A low Z story would have lacked Dick's coherence and general continuity of thought. Also, there might have been fewer pauses. There is an apparent lack of ambivalence. Zs can be highly ambivalent, but their ambivalences are of the "here today, there tomorrow" type rather than of the "here and now" type so common to the Ys.)

The purpose of this chapter has been to gather together some thoughts on the model which, hopefully, will clarify not only the four prototypes, A, X, Y, and Z, but also the two basic dimensions of the model, the developmental and the temperamental. Table 1. is offered as a summary of the four prototypes.

Interlude — An XYZ Preceptorial

Let us pause for a visit to an imaginary preceptorial in history. A preceptorial at Princeton is a small discussion group held weekly in addition to two lectures in a course. Faculty of all ranks serve as preceptors. This particular preceptorial is composed of students, x_1, x_2, x_3, y_1, y_2, z_1, and z_2.

The Nassau Hall bell has just stopped tolling and the preceptor is filling his pipe. The Xs are sitting with chairs slightly tilted back, heads resting lightly against the wall, eyes half closed. z_2, as usual, is absent. y_1 is asking z_1 how he did on last week's physics mid-term. z_1 replies (lying with a straight face) that he got a perfect paper. y_1 winces. z_1 smiles inwardly and stretches out his legs to the seat of the missing Z's chair. (Zs like to sprawl.)

x_1 knows he hasn't said a word in the precept yet this term. Preceptor structures a problem. y_2 leans forward to respond but y_1 beats him to it and points out, "But sir, life really isn't like that."

x_2 and x_3 watch attentively with chairs still tilted back. x_3 isn't worried. He said something last week.

x_1 begins to get an idea. z_1 is looking out the window, thoughts on last weekend. y_2 finally has his chance.

x_1 is mentally phrasing his idea. z_1 hears someone mention the name of his favorite Civil War general; he wheels about and gets into the discussion. y_1 and y_2 are still "with it."

TABLE I. *Characteristics of Students at Four Model Positions*

Prototype	A	X	Y	Z
Label	*Reasonable Adventurer*	*Non-committer*	*Hustler*	*Plunger*
Ego functioning	Integrative	Constricted	Semi-constricted	Dilated
Reactivity	Appropriate	Under-reactive	Counter-active	Over-reactive
Common defense	Reasoning	Denial	Reaction-formation	Apology, Restitution
Attitude toward instinctual self	Accepting	Unstructured	Rejecting	Alternating
Social motive	To communicate	To belong	To be esteemed	To be noticed
Regnant motive	To explore	To smooth over	To achieve	To create change
Problem	Frontier	Self expression	Self acceptance	Communication
Impression on others	Independent Sensitive Playful Compassionate	Bland Friendly Conforming Neutral	Aggressive Tough minded Cold Ambitious	Scattered Direct Impulsive Moody
Characteristic utterance	If only, then . . .	Who me?	Yes, but . . .	Why not!

x_1 is upset, as his thought is no longer relevant to the discussion; and he doubts whether it was a good idea anyway.

z_1 turns the subject back to his Civil War hero and mentions the very thought x_1 had. Preceptor praises z_1 for his "remarkable insight."

x_1 eyes z_1 and then slowly gathers up his books as the preceptorial comes to a close.

Chapter 5

Differential Development of Non-committers, Hustlers, and Plungers

Many in the Advisee Project did change in the course of four years. Some changed considerably. In terms of the developmental criteria of the model, the net change was in almost all instances for the better. One says "net" change because in six instances the sophomore year placement in the model was higher than that for the junior year. Figures 1 (p. 12), 14, 15 and 16 present the model positions of the students for freshman, sophomore, junior, and senior years respectively.

Figure 2 (p. 17) differentiates between those students graduating with honors and those graduating without honors. At Princeton honors are determined by vote of the faculty in a given department and based solely upon the student's performance on the senior thesis and final comprehensive examination of that department. Except for an established minimum, course grades are not considered. Figure 1 may be reviewed again in contrast with Figure 2. Note the relatively higher correlation between academic performance and level of development (as given by the model position) by the end of the senior year as compared to course grades and model position in the freshman year.

Figure 17 shows the course of development (or lack of development) of each student during his college career. It must seem paradoxical that instances of greatest amount of growth were among the Xs, a section of the

FIGURE 14.

Sophomore Year Model Positions

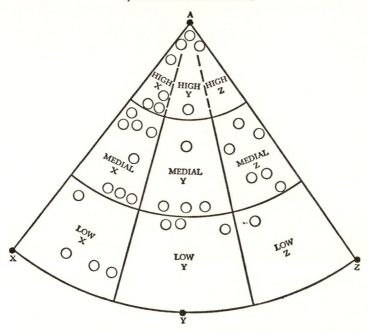

model in which *all* of the attrition occurred. The least amount of growth was represented by those who hovered over the Y point in the model. What is not apparent from these diagrams is *how* the student grew. Sustained observation of the students in the project convinced me that the factors associated with growth were highly differential in terms of temperament and level of development.

The Development of the Xs

The growth of the Xs was dependent upon two factors: moderate challenge and exposure to what I came to call "inner life activators." In regard to the first factor, challenge, X has a poor tolerance of anxiety but without

FIGURE 15.

Junior Year Model Positions

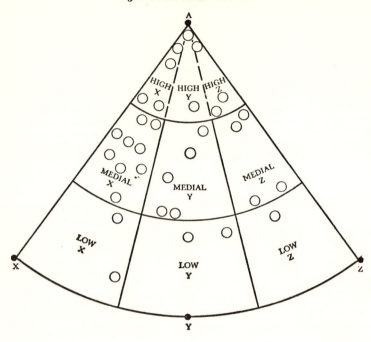

some anxiety he is unduly complacent. On the other hand, exposure to a high degree of pressure is not only enfeebling but also sets in motion unconscious defensive processes which leave him with an even more unfavorable educational stance. If he is well prepared for college, most of the challenges he will meet in the due course of academic work will be on a sufficient but moderate level. Most faculty advisers, I presume, take this factor of appropriate pacing into consideration at the time the student is consulting him in the selection of courses. If a personal tie is developed between the adviser and the student there should be ample opportunity to promote adequate challenges. As late as early senior year I recall asking three of

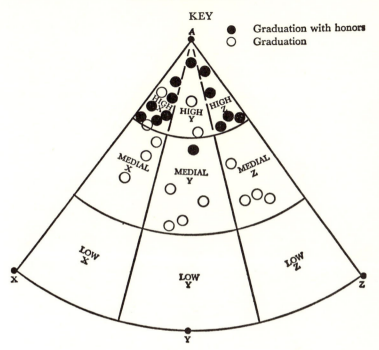

FIGURE 16.

Senior Year Model Positions

the students to come, individually, to my office for the purpose of posing for them a single question. All three were medial Xs and would have to maintain their C average in order to graduate. All three were literally shocked to hear me ask, "Do you realize that your chances of graduating are only fifty-fifty?" Each of them told me later that the jolt had induced him to do a bit of pondering. Once they started to think about it, they concluded that my probability figure was about correct.

Turning to the matter of inner-life activators the reader will recall our conception of X as a disconnected personality. Growth in X is a matter of reuniting the inner-

FIGURE 17.

Model Location Movement in College

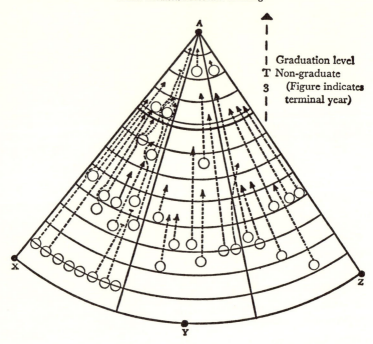

Graduation level
T Non-graduate
3 (Figure indicates terminal year)

self of fantasy with the outer-self of social and world interaction. X, therefore, is a difficult man to reach educationally. But, somehow, the humanities on impact operate to bypass the outer-self defenses and stimulate the inner-self. Art, music, and certain kinds of literature seem to arouse the deeper wishes, unfulfilled human strivings, to a point where they press up from within for expression.

For example, I recall a sophomore low medial X who once responded to my opening question of, "How are things going?" by saying, "I've been pretty busy, mentally at least."

"What do you mean, Ed?" I pursued.

"Well, I've been thinking," he said, "but the funny thing is that I'm not exactly sure what I have been thinking about."

"Perhaps you can tell me how all this thinking started," I suggested.

"It all goes back to English class last week. You see we have been reading *Moby Dick*. The old preacher gives a sermon to the whalers before they embark on a voyage. He said some things which kind of struck home and I've been thinking about it ever since."

Ed took out his copy of *Moby Dick* and pointed to a passage which he had underlined. It read, "Woe to him who seeks to pour oil upon the waters when God has brewed them into a gale! . . . Woe to him whose good name is more to him than goodness! Woe to him who, in this world, courts not dishonor! . . . Yea, woe to him who, as the great Pilot Paul has it, while preaching to others is himself a castaway!"

"This means something to me, somehow," Ed continued, "something really important."

We never did get a complete explanation from Ed of what this passage meant to him but perhaps that is unimportant. What is significant is that from that day in his English class, Ed began to reach for his education.

Consultation with a few of my teaching acquaintances in the field of literature yielded a goodly list of inner-life activators. I found these veteran teachers quite familiar with this phenomenon. There seemed to be general agreement that prose and poetry which deal heavily with the theme of contradiction in man's nature make the most promising inner-life activators. The list offered by some of my colleagues in English literature included:

DONNE   "Love of Religious Poetry"
               "Canonization"

DOSTOEVSKY	*The Brothers Karamazov*
	Crime and Punishment
ELIOT	*The Cocktail Party*
	"The Love Song of J. Alfred Prufrock"
	Murder in the Cathedral
EMERSON	*Essays*
FAULKNER	*Light in August*
HAWTHORNE	*The Scarlet Letter*
HUXLEY	*Brave New World*
KIERKEGAARD	"On Socrates"
MELVILLE	*Moby Dick*
NIEBUHR	*Moral Man and Immoral Society*
SALINGER	*Catcher in the Rye*
VEBLEN	*Theory of the Leisure Class*

Growth of the Xs was indicated by greater assertiveness and self-expression, by more willingness to risk an encounter. Those who reached the mid-point on the developmental dimension seemed to maintain at least this level or keep moving upward. For the others, their hold was indeed tenuous and subject to retrogression. A glance at Figure 17 will show that two men who started close to the bottom of the developmental scale made striking gains by senior year. The three ultimate academic failures, however, made little or no gain. What was the difference? The numbers are small and perhaps do not justify analytic comparisons. For what it is worth, an attempt was made to compare the two who did move up with the three who failed in freshman, sophomore, and junior year respectively. The initial clue was that the first group wrote home regularly and the second group did not. This fact lead me to another, viz., that the response to authority in the first group was ready and quick while this was not the case for the second group. The first group made serious attempts to study from the beginning while the study habits

THE REASONABLE ADVENTURER

of the other were erratic. The three families of the second group, however, shared the values of the families in the first group. All were deeply interested in the progress of their respective sons in college. The family demands on the second group, however, were met not with active rebellion, but with seeming acceptance and no response. In my opinion, psychological counseling with the second group would have met with equally poor response, at least in freshman year. One of the men, however, did wake up to his predicament in his junior year and actively sought help from me. He responded favorably to counseling but not in time to salvage him from a backlog of poor academic performances.

The Development of the Ys

My experience with the Ys convinces me that their development comes about in quite a different fashion than with Xs. This makes sense in terms of the theoretical picture of Y. It must be recalled that Y has erected about himself a defensive superstructure or pseudoself to protect him from his unwanted impulsive life. The content of this pseudoself in terms of self-concept and attitude toward life is the antithesis of the basic self he is rejecting.[1] As long as Y comes close to fulfilling his pseudoself through attaining high grades, money, social status, good morals, or whatever, there is little likelihood of his giving serious consideration to coming to terms with himself. He must go down before he can go up.

Relevant to this dilemma of the Y was a student in the Advisee Project whom I shall call Fred. Like many Ys, Fred came to college fresh from a high school "wheeldom"

---

1. Manes Sperber must have had in mind a Y when he wrote of a certain kind of person, "The pose, the mask, the borrowing gesture, fleeting as they may be, reveal what a man wishes to seem and by antithesis what he does not wish to be, and therefore what he really is."

and a record of high aptitude scores and good grades. He came also with three ambitions. He wanted to play varsity football, first team. He also wanted to be president of his class. Finally, he wanted to enter in his junior year the School of Public and International Affairs (the Woodrow Wilson School) in preparation for a career in the foreign service, perhaps to be an ambassador some day.

In freshman football Fred was the first one out on the playing field for each day of practice. If practice was scheduled for four o'clock Fred would be there at three. He worked hard but he had been trained for the T formation. Princeton plays single wing. For his position the difference was a critical one. He had difficulty getting beyond the third team. The coach said he couldn't get Fred to relax. Consequently he was not asked to come out for varsity football training in the fall of his sophomore year. One down and two to go.

Class elections were held in the spring of Fred's freshman year. In spite of studious efforts to connect names with the faces of his classmates he ran last in the elections.

Those who wish to major in the School of Public and International Affairs must pass screening by a faculty committee of that school. Course grades through the middle of sophomore year must be high in order to be considered. Fred made good grades freshman year but could not cope with his sophomore courses which demanded more originality and flexibility of thinking. First term sophomore year was a nightmare for Fred. Up to then he had lived with an abiding faith that plain hard work would be sufficient to keep him on top academically. He worked late each night, rarely leaving the study room in the library before closing time, midnight. He was now facing an awful truth: Fellow classmates were working less hard and procuring better grades than he. In March he was notified by the Woodrow Wilson School that he was not one of the fifty in his class selected. Reason: poor grades.

Fred, as they say, "had had it." He came to my office visibly upset. The staunch controls were gone, his defenses down. For the first time I came to know Fred well. In the subsequent sessions that we arranged Fred made a determined effort to review his life faithfully and get to the bottom of things. In this effort to see and live with his total self he was largely successful. We did not talk about study habits, nor did we discuss vocational goals. My concern centered, rather, on Fred's acceptance of his deeper impulses and feelings.

In the latter half of the second semester I saw a marked improvement in Fred's academic performance. Also, his social relationships were becoming more relaxed and natural. One day in June I received a phone call from Professor Lockwood of the Woodrow Wilson School. There was an opening for one more student and he asked about Fred. Fred was notified of his acceptance shortly thereafter.

The reconstruction of a Y apparently requires a calamity. In Fred's case the architect for the calamity was the liberal arts program itself—its residential setting and demands for originality and reflective thinking. Without a fall the Y is a hard man to help by means of counseling and psychotherapy. To use a Christian analogy, he must experience Good Friday before Easter.

Unless the demands of the education program are high and unrelenting in the area of creative thinking, the Y may complete college without a crisis and therefore remain unreconstructed. Another unhappy possibility is that the Y may achieve a position of prominence in an athletic or other extracurricular activity. Such a status might feed the needs of the pseudoself (the reaction-formation) and thereby thwart the possibility of a liberating education.

Must there be a crisis? Is there no alternative to cracking the rigid superstructure of the Y? I believe there is an effective alternative to bringing a Y to terms with himself other than through a situational crisis. Instead of effecting a blow one can apply heat and *melt* the pseudoself. The opportunity to melt a Y is not easy to arrange, however. One evening during the junior year of the Advisee Project, I rearranged the composition of one of the regular project discussion groups to include one Y, two Xs and five Zs. It was a lively evening with beer and pretzels, and it lasted well into the small hours of the morning. Y opened the meeting in his customary manner and was soon placed in the position of defending his dogmatic statements. The Zs were taunting him but as the evening wore on there was genuine warmth in their taunts. To this, Y began reciprocating in kind. By the end of the meeting we had two Xs and six Zs. Our Y had melted.

Y was back to his old self the next day but the experience of that evening provided a clue to a promising method for promoting growth in the Y. The technique requires a sustained exposure to love and affection. Our Y, in my opinion, shed his pseudoself that evening because he came to sense in others a response to his genuine self. He found they were liking him as a human being. Exposure of the real self failed to elicit the rejection he deeply feared. The pseudoself, therefore, was rendered useless. Many more such experiences would be required because the past is deeply engrained in Y. He is not easily convinced.

Once Y *is* convinced that he is valued as a human being in his own right, it is an event of paramount importance to his development. In fact, one student in the project, an erstwhile low medial Y, pinpointed the upturn in his development at a time in the second semester of his sophomore year when a young lady came to accept him fully and value him dearly. He later spoke of this period in his final senior year interview: "All these emotional things . . . not being accepted and having to prove myself through extracurricular stuff and high grades, these were just props. In high school it was just one prop, one false front, after another. Then, about two years ago everything just sort of dropped away. I began to look at all of me instead of looking at just half of me. It was then that I started to grow up."

The Y is well worth saving. Through reconstruction he loses his intellectual rigidity, social insensitivity, and obsessive drive. He can be expected, however, to retain a capacity for three things: hard work, staunch adherence to his values, and a good fight. When tinged with a little Z-ness he makes an excellent college president.

The Development of the Zs

The Zs, a relatively small group, can wear out more faculty members than all the other groups combined. They are good "idea men" and do not take kindly to criticism of their overly ambitious schemes. In consulting you they rarely make appointments but walk right in, eager to flood you with the details of their newly found ideas. In these states of excitement they are apparently oblivious to the thought that you might have something better or more important to do with your time. In my experience there is no real solution to the problem. Even if you hide, the Zs will be sure to find you.

But if you stay with the Z student, you have a friend. I believe it is important for his growth that he have such a friend, either his adviser or some other faculty member to whom he has taken a liking. If a close association can be sustained for at least a semester, then that relationship can serve a valuable function as a kind of external reality base about which Z can begin to integrate the many aspects of his college career. He is difficult to understand but important inroads of understanding can be made if he is given a hearing over a period of time.

The Z deeply needs a person who has come to tolerate and understand his wide swings of mood. There may be times of depression, for example, when he might do something rash. It is not so much that he might take his life (for Ys are greater suicide risks) but that he might take an irrevokable step such as quitting college. Usually a quiet word advising him to postpone action for a day or so will be sufficient to tide him over to the arrival of a better mood.

As I have indicated, Z is a strong individualist. He is, therefore, more likely to grow in a residential climate that is tolerant of expressions of individuality, odd as he might seem to be. His apartness from the mainstream is not so much that others disapprove of his eccentricities (which may be the case) but that they do not understand him.

Whether it be in conference, recitations, papers, or examinations, the instructors of a Z should make a special effort to demand coherence. Z characteristically neglects to clothe his ideas in a framework that would make his utterances comprehensible to others. In class discussion he often zips from one idea to another with the result that he baffles his audience regarding the point that he is trying to make.

In spite of the fact that those who resided on the Z side of the model had on the average the lowest College Board aptitude scores [2] they completed their senior year with the best grades. To me this is partially understandable because, while they may have scattered their energies in the underclass years, they usually found their niche by

2. I also have a suspicion that Zs do relatively poorly on multiple choice or true and false tests because of the dissociative trend in their thinking.

junior year. When this happened their academic career took on greater form.

The stabilization of form in the growing Z is highly dependent upon a process which might be called the externalization of the internal criterion. The Z may develop rapidly in an atmosphere of a few understanding teachers and friends. Such gains, however, may rest on precarious ground unless the Z is successful in finding a broad philosophical framework which provides a loom for the poorly integrated threads of the inner-self. Michael, I believe, was successful in this. An externalization or objectification of a sentiment was indicated when he remarked in his final senior interview, "I was always for Roosevelt but now I know why I was for Roosevelt." (See Michael's final senior interview in Appendix A.)

Summation

In summary, we see X, Y, and Z as dependent upon respectively different features of college life for their growth and development. If all goes well X becomes more lively and self-directed; Y becomes more human, more deeply self-accepting, more flexible; and Z becomes more settled and comprehensible to others. As these students approach the A point in the model their life becomes more open to new experience. They are then ready to prepare themselves to be well informed and discriminating persons and thus fully benefit from graduate or professional training.

The primary need of the Reasonable Adventurer in the project was *access* to a variety of frontiers. This, I believe, they had at Princeton in good measure. They had access to many books, well-equipped laboratories, and growing men as teachers. And perhaps the greatest opportunity of all was the companionship of other Reasonable Adventurers.

Chapter 6

The Seniors View Their Development in College[1]

The final interview of senior year was an appropriate time for a summing up. Much of it was devoted to eliciting from each of the remaining twenty-eight men a comparison of two personal images: the student as a freshman and as a senior after four years in college. These reports when viewed *in toto* offer a lively commentary regarding the growth of the Advisee Project as a whole. The changes noted in the students from freshman to senior year vary according to the different aspects of their lives. The topical sequence used in the final senior interview ran as follows: intellectual, social, family relationships, political attitudes, and finally religious feeling and outlook. Where possible, a student's verbatim statement from this interview is used to describe the developmental trend noted.

Anyone who uses the term "intellectual" with a group of Princeton freshmen does so at his own risk. Intellectuals, they would say, are like people who go to Harvard. By sophomore year "intellectual activity" becomes somewhat respectable, but "an intellectual" lingers in disrepute. Through junior and senior year the intellectual is progressively seen as more worldly, more manly, more useful in society, and less a species all of his own. At any rate, by senior year I judged it was relatively safe to ask the members of the Advisee Project about their intellectual

1. This chapter appeared in substantially the same form in the October 15, 1955, issue of the *Princeton Alumni Weekly*.

development and whether or not they would send their son to Harvard. Incidentally, some said they would.

In the twenty-eight respective statements regarding intellectual change the most frequently expressed notion was the shift in motivation for academic pursuit. Not more than five or six of the project members claimed for themselves as freshmen a genuine thirst for knowledge in its own right. Work was viewed as something externally directed, as an obligation, as a means to an end. By senior year at least three quarters of them revealed that studying had become a pleasure, something intrinsically interesting. The way in which this change was expressed is, I think, of sufficient interest to quote rather extensively. If there is a bias in my selection of statements,[2] it is in the direction of the student's eloquence. Here are some statements typical of others in that they indicate the nature of the change in motivation for college work:

1. "I am much more involved, more interested, more captivated by my work than I was freshman year when it was just a chore to be done. I never thought I'd really get interested in school work. Now I find I can."

2. "I enjoy sitting down and reading a book and trying to grasp what the author is saying whereas before it was done as an assignment."

3. "There are more things all the time that become pleasures instead of duties."

4. "The biggest change in my intellectual life is the desire to read—everything in general. I now find satisfaction in reading, which is something I never had before."

2. The reader should know that few of the students quoted in this chapter have had any opportunity to see their oral statements in writing. The writer has adhered to the verbatim transcript except for occasionally inserting connectives in the interest of coherence. Care has been taken not to include material that would identify the student quoted. Each paragraph in a section of quotations represents a different student.

5. "Coming in you find out there is so much you didn't know that you are almost driven to read this and then read that and then go on to read that and that and that. Now it's not so much a drive anymore as trying to get the maximum out of what you do read. . . . The appetites created here enable you to read more intelligently and give you a desire to read more."

6. "I think the change has been a more natural interest —almost excitement in certain areas of study . . . anthropology, religion, politics, even history I'm beginning to get a feel for. Others which I didn't push through at all I really have an interest in—things like art and architecture. Now I can see how I could get enjoyment by becoming wrapped up in any of them. A lot I know I'll never get too damn deep into but I'll still sort of enjoy them all along the way."

The statements just quoted represent the main drift of the changes reported but hardly do justice to the diversity found in the replies. To this end I am including at some length the statements of six members, all of whom felt a change but described this change differently:

1. "In freshman and sophomore year it was get all the knowledge you can, followed by a cynical, skeptical what's the use of it all. In my freshman and sophomore years I wanted to discover what somebody else had to say. In junior and senior year I wanted to throw it all out of the window and start saying what I felt like saying. The first thing I want to do after Princeton is to write a story."

2. "Professor Harbison put it well when he corrected one of my examinations: 'You have a great knowledge of facts but you do not interpret them well.' I would say that was my freshman year in a nutshell; it was high school, grade 13. . . . I was hesitant at first to assert

my own opinion of things, to present my ideas for somebody else to bat around. This is the first time I have come to real conviction. That has been the change; and it has affected sorta—everything."

3. "My intellectual life is about the same. I'll put it this way, I'm never gonna be one of those intensely inquisitive guys that would pick up a book on Hegel or Karl Marx. I don't think I've changed *that* much. But this is what Princeton has done for me: It's thrown a lot of stuff at me that I have absorbed in such a way that I now have certain things I want to do in later life. . . . Just being around a guy like Professor Isely made me interested in reading more about the Civil War. Also, from some of the medieval history that I've been exposed to more or less by accident, everytime I see a book on some guy's shelf about the decline and fall of the Roman Empire, it interests me somewhat. I always pick it up and look through it. So I'd say in summary that . . . I've gotten a great deal out of it. My intellectual curiosity will never change. I'm more interested in other things."

4. "The change for me has been a diminution of the intellectual life. I mean by 'intellectual': unattached to philosophical thought, that is thought which is usually no more than a chess game with words—I look upon words as kind of labels that can be thrown away or attached to objects. You can take the labels off everything around you, and retire into a cell and shuffle them. Only a few months ago did I begin to come out, I think, and could re-attach the labels to the objects. It's really a kind of travesty to use the word 'chair' without having one right with you, if you see what I mean. That's Plato's mistake, all the way through. He imagines just because he has an idea of a triangle, therefore

the label 'triangle' must be floating up in the air. Because he sees that no triangle can be made on earth that's perfect, he floats it up there somewhere."

5. "I think the freshman year phase, which was a carry-over from the prep-school phase, was a period of just trying to do things for the sake of getting them done, looking at intellectual things as something to get out of the way before playing tennis or going on a weekend. That is, the ideas themselves were not really important. From sophomore year until perhaps the middle of this year, ideas became increasingly important. But now I am becoming increasingly utilitarian in my outlook. I am still aware of the importance of ideas but I realize that the most important thing for me to do is to learn to become a doctor, that I am a much richer and deeper person for having this background of intellectual concern and knowledge . . . not as an end in itself but in its applicability to what I am going to do in life."

6. "I don't really know. It is hard to remember how I felt freshman year. I was going to say that perhaps I gained a deeper appreciation of the arts. Of course, I gained a deeper appreciation of the sciences because that is what I have been studying primarily. . . . I think I probably got as much satisfaction out of my humanities as a freshman as I did, say, from the architecture course that I am taking this spring term. I think it is one of the most wonderful courses I've taken here in the University. . . . I found that buildings just interest me, much more so than poetry. I never realized I had the interest before but it is perfectly rational when you get right down to it. Nothing fascinates me more than structure and function. The connection between my scientific courses and an art course such as architecture is very, very evident. When you study modern architecture and begin to investigate the latest engineer-

ing principles you also find in your studies of vertebrate anatomy that Nature has really outdone the engineers."

Peer Relationships

The changes reported in the areas of human relationships do not permit as general a finding as did the changes in intellectual development. It makes considerable difference whether the discussion refers to relations with their peers (persons of the same age and sex), with girls, or with the immediate family. In the sphere of peer relationships half of the project members stressed the change as being primarily improvement in the nature of their casual relationships. These men said that as freshmen they did not feel comfortable with the associates that were beyond the inner circle of friends, and that their relations with those whom they did not know well became easier, more enjoyable, and more tolerant. For example, one student in the group said:

"I have always had the capacity for deep friendship but I never was able to maintain a lot of casual relationships in addition to the deeper ones. I think I have learned to do that particularly this year. In other words, I have a lot more of what I call good acquaintances at the club . . . people that I am perfectly comfortable with playing bridge and so forth."

Another group, a third of the project, stressed the changes as being in the formation of new close friendships. Some of them had never realized before what a rich experience such a friendship can be; others felt their criterion of friendship had changed. One quotation in particular illustrates this:

"I have been narrowing more and more whereas earlier I was trying to broaden the number of friends. I think now that there is more emphasis on fundamental beliefs . . . or the enjoyment we get out of looking at each other's completely different ideas. The basis for friendship is different in a way. It is not based on outward achievement in athletic success or success in any particular area but more on the type of person, the way he views other people and the way he approaches his problems. I mean it has become really important that a person's ideas have been found out by his own thought and not by someone else's and important that a person be really open-minded and not dogmatic for any sort of deep friendship. The change that has come is the realization that . . . if you really want to be a close friend of someone, you have to listen to his ideas and give your own in return. You have to appreciate other people's points of view more than I think I did. I was probably more selfish in my freshman year. I did not appreciate the joys you can have in friendships. . . . It has been a deep and rich thing."

The remaining five members of the project felt no change in their peer relations. Some of them wished matters would improve, others felt their relationships were satisfactory from the beginning.

Women

The matter of association with the opposite sex is not so encouraging. One would gather from the twenty-eight statements that half of the project took a dim view of their relationship with women their own age. The other half were more optimistic in this report. The distinction between the two groups, however, is more gradual than precise. For some reason those who took the dim view tended to be more eloquent in their statements. To quote some:

1. "I'd say I'm still pretty pessimistic about girls. . . . Perhaps I'm a little more charitable when it comes to making out."

2. "My relationships with girls are not good. . . . I haven't had enough experience, actually."

3. "I've come a long ways but have a heck of a long way to go yet."

4. "I now have very definite opinions about what to expect from a girl. Very seldom find it."

5. "No change, no date in four years."

6. "Never really got straightened out; never found a deep personal relationship with a girl but it is something that will come in time."

7. "I don't understand girls. I used to think I did. . . . The girls you see are interested in finding a man. They are always painted up and so forth. You are not going to find much that is natural and wholesome in a girl, particularly on a weekend down here. My conclusion from that is that girls have rather weak characters in the sense that they feel like they have to come down here and conform to something."

The statements of the remaining half of the project reflected more satisfaction with their relationships with women of their age. Some of these reported no changes but, on the other hand, were not unhappy about the *status quo*. Others felt matters had changed for the better. None of the students had married prior to graduation but five did so within the first year after college. All five of these, it should be said, tended to take the brighter view.

Family Relationships

When it came to family relationships twenty-one of the twenty-eight students claimed a definite change for the better. Thirteen of these expressed it in terms of becoming closer to the family in general. Such statements as these are typical:

1. "I have come to appreciate how fortunate I am in having the family I do have."

2. "Relationships with the family much better. I see that I did not include them as much as I could in what I was really doing at college."

3. "My family and I have reached an understanding. They have come to appreciate I'm a senior now which has been a very hard struggle for them. But I think they have done very well."

The remaining eight of the twenty-one stressed, in particular, the improved relationship with the head of the family. Some said, for instance:

1. "There's been a lot more interaction between my father and me . . . rather [than] hiding things . . . not bringing up problems. . . ."

2. "Understand the old man more. I used to think he was pretty much a Greek god."

3. "As for my father I idealized him as a freshman. Every minute that I have been here he has become more and more of a human being. There's more give and take in the relationship and I see his faults and everything. . . . I've become a lot more independent of the family, which essentially means Papa."

The other members of the project either saw no change or what change they did note they viewed with misgiving. For example, some sensed a growing distance in communication brought about in part by the increased gap in educational level, or through simply being away from home for so long a period.

Political Interest

In the political area twenty-one felt that there had been a change and much of the change was expressed in terms of greater interest. In respect to the direction of the change the movement was toward the center politically. By senior year the right wing of the Republican party was represented by only one student ("I came in here a Republican and I leave here a Republican"). The left wing of the Democratic party was not represented at all, even though at least one or two students would have placed themselves there in their underclass years. Many said that they had become more concerned with international affairs in particular. Two students were seriously considering entering politics. Only five students disclaimed any interest in politics at any time.

Religion

When I came to the area of religion my questions were designed to elicit material bearing on two dimensions. First, the students were asked whether there had been any change in the degree of involvement, the extent to which religion was a meaningful and important aspect of their life. Second, they were asked whether there had been any change in the *nature* of their religious outlook, their concept of God and the institution of the church. According to their reports, only two of the twenty-eight students felt that there had been any change in the *level* of involvement, and both of these felt a deepening of interest in religion during the four years at college. There were no statements made which reflected a genuine religious conversion, although one came close.

For eight students, religion was a matter to which they were emotionally indifferent all during college. Eighteen claimed a personal interest in religion when entering college and had maintained essentially the same level of involvement throughout the four years. Two, as we said, felt an increase in involvement. Within the group three levels of involvement were represented: moderate (three students), high (eight students), and very high (seven students). In other words, if a student arrived on the campus involved in religion he left involved; if he arrived indifferent to religion, as did eight, he left indifferent.

Some may feel that increased religious involvement ought to be one of the products of a liberal arts education.

They may be wondering whether the eight students who remained indifferent to religion while at college tended to be among those that Princeton did not reach in general. However, three of the eight graduated with high honors and two with honors. Since thirteen of the Advisee Project were honor graduates, the eight religiously uninvolved students compared favorably, at least against the criterion of scholarship. Some readers might be impressed, on the other hand, that twenty students had at least maintained their involvement in religion.

As for changes in religious outlook, we are reduced to considering the remarks of the twenty involved students. Of those, fourteen felt their outlook had changed. Some are quoted to indicate the direction of the change that many seemed to imply:

1. "It is more individualistic . . . pretty much my own, I don't share it with anybody."

2. "I've come to not place so much importance on the ritual. . . . I am trying to find a liaison, so to speak, between myself and God, and I am not sure the Episcopalian church is it. However, it might be. I'm not sure any church is it."

3. "I feel a great oneness with the idea of the complete depravity of man and his complete inability to do anything to save himself. . . . This is a very definite change, because earlier I put a great deal of stock in virtue, human endeavor, but I don't any more; I don't mean when I say this that I could become a Calvinist. I don't want to be isolated in anything. I want to be maneuverable in everything in my life. I don't want to be set in one position. . . ."

4. "I had definite religious training and I understand, I think, what it means to have a good religious background such as I had at [prep] school for five years. . . . But starting with my sophomore year in college,

a very decided disworldliness has taken place, so that the religious outlook as it now stands is such that I could accept a religious experience, but it can not be a conventional one. It will not be a conventional one. . . . What I would be looking for would be a very intense personal faith or something."

From the religious changes which the religiously involved group reported it is clear that many were still searching for a relationship with God or the mystery of being. But they had come to a point where they wanted to bypass the conventional ways of establishing this commitment. Our established churches were somehow seen as part of the provincial world which they had come to suspect. During a phase of their life when their perspective was continuing to widen, dogma and doctrine were words that became distasteful as connoting confinement rather than expression. The very nature of their education left them suspended on some important life issues, but at least the issues had been raised.

The Value of a Residential College

The experience of reviewing the conferences of that spring of 1954 has reinforced a conviction that grew within me during the four years of the Advisee Project. It is that the residential life offered on the campus was one of the important factors in bringing about the intellectual and social development reflected in the statements of the twenty-eight seniors. The students at Princeton live together. To an amazing extent they inspire each other. This, in my opinion, would not be possible without an able student body, the curricular demands for quality and sustained effort, and last but by no means least the cloistered living. This brings to mind Joyce Cary's words on the Oxford of his younger days: "What one remembers is that withdrawn quietness and the long evenings of talk among friends in some room still further withdrawn —at a double remove from city bustle and the casual intruder.

. . . .

The mere sense of being crowded prevents reflection. And reflection, leisure, are at the very roots of a true education—not only to acquire knowledge but to think it over and especially to have plenty of that kind of absorbed talk which is thinking aloud." [3]

The cloister connotes detachment from reality. One can not, however, confront all of reality at once. A thorough examination of the past requires at least a temporary respite from pressing problems of the present. How else is a balanced perspective to be achieved? Relative isolation in college is an important, if not necessary, precursor of a student's full and meaningful participation in contemporary affairs to come.

3. Joyce Cary, "The Oxford Scholar," *Holiday*, XIII, No. 6 (June 1953), p. 96.

Chapter 7

Implications for Higher Education

What does all this mean for higher education? What implications can be drawn from this study for our colleges and universities today? As I see it there are several. The first has to do with the development of Reasonable Adventurers.

The principal value judgment of this study is the exalted position of the Reasonable Adventurer. He stands at the apex of the developmental scale. Does this mean that the primary objective of a college is the production of Reasonable Adventurers? It is true that for some colleges the stated institutional goal is clearly developmental. They want to produce mature minds. We repeat John Witherspoon's dictum that "the end of a liberal education is to set all human powers in motion." Yet one wonders if Dr. Witherspoon would have proposed to his faculty the granting of the baccalaureate degree to a freshman who was judged to have already attained the status of a Reasonable Adventurer. Most faculty members, I believe, would react to the case with a general rejoicing at the discovery of this fellow and declare him "truly ready for college." Here we encounter implicitly the other frequently stated objective, the absorption of the wisdom of the past. The distinction, however, between the developmental and absorptive objectives is somewhat academic. On the one hand we accept the idea of preparing individuals to educate themselves. On the other hand we grant that the very process of meaningfully connecting an individual with his heritage is, if successful, a liberating experience for student and teacher alike. Perhaps we can agree on this: A college or university that does not generate Reasonable Adventurers is not engaged in higher education.

The presence of Reasonable Adventurers among the student body can do much to set in motion a healthy academic climate. Their interaction with each other can make intellectual activity on the campus fashionable and thereby promote the development of many who are ready to move intellectually. This kind of outcome is too precious to be left to chance. There is much that colleges and universities can do in the way of unseen support. For example, Knox College assigns dormitory space with its Reasonable Adventurers in mind. The most promising freshmen are given rooms near each other, a cluster here and a cluster there. Knox finds that such groups not only sustain themselves but in time "corrupt" others.

Now that I have joined the ranks of those who value Reasonable Adventurers, what are the prospects? How many can we expect to have among our entering freshmen; how many more can we expect to produce within four years of college? If the Princeton study is a sufficient guide, the prospects are sobering. Seven students were judged to be Reasonable Adventurers in their freshman year. This number rose to sixteen or 45 per cent, if the two instances of death remained in the count of Reasonable Adventurers. All of this took place in a context of one of the most selective student bodies and most intensive educational programs in the country. We are not likely to be deceiving ourselves if we conclude that the proportion of Reasonable Adventurers among our graduating senior classes in this country is running far short of one-half.

Producing Reasonable Adventurers is an expensive and

time-consuming affair. Many professional schools have come to require at least two years of liberal arts as a base for the professional training to come. Others have moved to graduate programs exclusively. I wonder how two years of liberal training could be sufficient. Woodrow Wilson, when he was president of Princeton, once participated in a debate on this issue. Apparently some of those present were arguing that a two-year liberal arts experience was a sufficient antecedent to the specialized curricula of the professional schools of law, medicine, and the ministry. To them Woodrow Wilson replied: "I take it for granted that those who have formulated the proposals really never knew a sophomore in the flesh. The sap of manhood is rising in him but it has not yet reached his head." A two-year liberal arts program is probably less adequate today than in Wilson's time. For most undergraduates four years of liberal arts are necessary for any education worthy of the name "liberal." Even this length of time may not be sufficient but it is well worth the try. Certainly compression of the college curriculum to less than four years could be cause for concern. If we succeed in producing a Reasonable Adventurer, we have a precious outcome—a generalist who can evaluate ends as well as produce means.

The Place of the Humanities

There are two findings of this study that speak more directly to the curriculum builders in our colleges and universities. The first is the special place of the enlivening arts; the second is the importance of curricular demands for a sustained and, at times, exhaustive effort on the part of the student.

As to the humanities, they speak to the core of the individual. They spark the inner reaches to set in motion the imaginative processes of all but the most hardened. The study of art, music, literature, philosophy, and religion may seem vague, even useless, in a materialistic culture. But their impact is by no means intangible to those who are priviledged to witness or experience the inner-life activation that follows. The humanities in this study were one of the few aspects of the curriculum that succeeded in getting Xs moving, and Xs are a sizeable group. For the Ys, the writing of essays required in literature courses, when deftly handled by the instructor, did much to bring them into a more direct encounter with their alien inner-selves and thereby set the stage for change. As Emerson once said, "In every work of genius we recognize our own rejected thoughts; they come back to us with a certain alienated majesty." Even the Zs, certainly in no need of inner-life activation, found in the great works not only a kindred soul or two but often a framework within which to deal with the world confronting them.

Too often one hears the place of English in the curriculum justified by various references to the value of learning to speak and write clearly. Sometimes I suspect that this is the *only* rationale at some institutions for including English in an engineering curriculum. If we are looking for groups that need their inner-life ruffled, let us not forget the freshman engineers!

In proclaiming the critical importance of the humanities to the full development of our young men and women, I in no way wish to discount their importance in childhood. How much better it is if the art and literature in college can hark back to a rich and abiding imaginative life experienced in childhood.

The Demand for a Sustained Effort

Our students, once cocked and set in motion, may never acquire form and identity unless they are challenged to set down their ideas in a meaningful framework. In this regard, the senior thesis becomes a proper keystone to a college career. Upon reviewing the lives of the men in the Advisee Project it is hard to isolate an experience that engendered more honest self-respect than the completion of the senior thesis. Except for the student and the faculty supervisor, these are seldom read by others, even though some may be deserving of a wider audience. Once completed, the role of the thesis in the upperclass curriculum program is largely fulfilled. It is clearly the heaviest single academic demand in college. The effort required is in itself an obstacle. Pushing a pencil for forty to a hundred thousand words is an accomplishment that few have experienced. Also it is a highly personal task for the student. No one can rightfully do it for him. Without its satisfactory completion he cannot be graduated. With a thesis well done, he has a right to be proud of himself.

Colleges that fail to require a major production such as the thesis are missing, to my way of thinking, a fine curricular instrument for the growth and development of their students. Some offer the chance to write a thesis but do not require it. It is hard to imagine that a student fully recognizes the value of completing a thesis until he has completed one. So why give the student the choice? Offering a choice assumes not only that the student possesses at this stage an understanding of its real worth but also that he possesses the strength of character to assign himself the task. Granted that some students are mature enough to meet these criteria, this still in all probability leaves behind in the ranks a host of those who need the experience just as much, perhaps even more.

Extracurricular Activities

My next area of indulgence is the place of extracurricular activities. Perhaps they have a place, perhaps they do not. I have come, at any rate, to the view that each extracurricular activity can stand close scrutiny regarding its place in the overall educational scheme if for no other reason than they are so time consuming. I post no argument against such expressive activities as campus theaters, literary magazines, mountaineering clubs, debating, and informal discussion groups. To single out two activities that do seem questionable, however, I would like to say a few words about student government and the campus newspaper.

The problem with these two endeavors is that they are so seductive. Their place on the campus carries such an appearance of legitimacy that the participating student comes easily to the conclusion that he is doing something worthwhile. While it is tenable that student councils and newspapers perform an honest and valued service to the campus, the rewards to the participants themselves may not be so enduring. The question must be asked by students so engaged, "Is *this* what I ought to be doing with my time?" The answer is not easy, particularly for those selected for these duties by classmates or administrative officers. There is often the soul searching problem of conflicting loyalties. It is not easy for a given student to set aside the urgings of his classmates that he run for office, or the expressed wishes of a dean that he assume editorial duties with the daily newspaper. Here is the time for the student to be selfish and look to his own intellectual development. He may not pass this way again.

If we exclude the quasi-professional athletics current on some campuses, the place of organized and informal athletics is not easily questioned. This is especially the case where team participation is not heavily status-involving. It is an individual matter but most students do seem to benefit from engaging in regular strenuous exercise and at least some form of personal contact sport. To me one of the most impressive scenes at Princeton was the late afternoon exodus to the playing fields.

Differences in Temperament and Level of Development
Perhaps the clearest lesson learned from this study of thirty-six students is that the effectiveness of a particular method of teaching, advising, or counseling is likely to be differential among the students. It may vary considerably according to both the temperament and the level of development of the student. What is growth enhancing for a Y, for example, may be enfeebling for an X. In the area of counseling, a non-directive technique is tailor made for a medial X but a waste of time for a medial Y. Not only does our experience in counseling the two groups support this view but I now think we have the beginning of a rationale as to why this must be so. The day may not be far off when measures of personality and level of development are included in our college orientation testing programs. What is more, we may even know then what to do with the test scores.

Participation in the Advisee Project
The students in the Advisee Project had an element in their college career not shared by their classmates. This element, of course, was their participation in the project itself. Any program which required on the average ten hours per semester of each man's time should be a potential factor in their development for better or for worse. When one realizes the highly personal nature of the project the impact may have been considerable. What evidences do we have?

The life of a student at Princeton is highly competitive. To a large extent the students themselves are responsible for this. It is not likely, therefore, that a student would consent to demands such as this project required had the program been disruptive. As it turned out not a single member of the study asked to drop out. He may have considered doing so but if he did I was not aware of it. Why did they continue? Since I never asked this question directly, I can only make a few conjectures. Perhaps one reason was idealism. Many must have felt that a university should be actively assessing its own program, and were therefore willing to do what they could to help. These men, for the most part, were highly idealistic. The problem was, how to express it appropriately. The Advisee Project, I believe, offered them an opportunity to make their idealism explicit. Another reason they may have continued grew out of the personal relationship with the adviser. I had the tremendous advantage of time. Where the other underclass advisers normally could allot only three hours a week to sixty advisees, I could spend thirty hours a week with thirty-six advisees. We came in most instances to know and trust each other, and from this kind of relationship a large measure of satisfaction was gained. In short, they seemed to enjoy a relationship in which they could discuss matters freely.

Perhaps a more objective indication of the specific effect of the project on the participants is made available through a comparison of outcomes between the Advisee Project and its control group. At the very onset of the study thirty-one of the project members were paired with a non-project classmate of similar family and educational background; in other words, with another representative sample of the class. Table 2 displays the outcome of this comparison in terms of attrition and academic honors. Except for the deaths (two of three in the class) and disciplinary dismissals the difference is in favor of the Advisee Project.

A comparison of extracurricular participation is also interesting. The comparison group slightly exceeded, on the average, the number of specific activities listed. But the Advisee Project far exceeded the control group in the number of top leadership positions held. For example, in the senior year the Advisee Project could list among its members three varsity captains, the chairman, vice chairman, and secretary of the undergraduate council, the president of the debating halls, and the head of the campus radio station.

TABLE 2.

Comparison in Outcome of Advisee Project and Its Control Group

	Advisee Project	Comparison Group
Number of matched cases	31	31
Deaths	2	0
Academic dismissals	1	6
Disciplinary dismissals	2	0
Withdrawals	1	4
Total Attrition	6	10
Graduation *Cum Laude*	6	2
Magna Cum Laude	6	3
Summa Cum Laude	1	0
Total Honors	13	5

I was talking with a senior one Friday evening very late in May. He had just taken his senior comprehensives on Monday, Tuesday, and Wednesday but now he was cleaned up and seemed well rested. Obviously thinking back on this whole business of college, he said, "You know, if Princeton has not done anything else for me it has made me more aware, a hell of a lot more aware."

The enhancement of awareness. This is our story.

Postscript—Nine Years Later

As this book goes to press, a quick follow-up on the thirty-four Project members is in order. We now know where each man is residing and what he is doing. Less than a year from now will be their tenth college reunion. With military service and professional training out of the way, the majority have been settled into a career for only a year or so.

All but two project members are college graduates. Twenty-four project members pursued a graduate or professional program beyond their Princeton undergraduate work. Only one member remained at Princeton for graduate work. Four are Ph.Ds. Incidentally, all four were classified as Reasonable Adventurers by senior year. The first to receive his Ph.D. was one of four Reasonable Adventurers according to freshman year placement in the model. Throughout he was top man in the model but, interestingly, in the lowest third of the project in both college boards and freshman grade average (see Figures 3 and 4).

All but two are or were married. Two are now divorced.

Table 3, Occupational and Marital Status of Advisee Project, is offered as a summary of the group's present status with regard to occupation and marital status. The

TABLE 3.

Occupational and Marital Status of Advisee Project—Nine Years Later

TEMPERAMENT	X	Y	Z	TOTAL
OCCUPATION				
Scholar	3	1	1	5
Business	6	3	2	11
Law	3	1	1	5
Medicine	2	2	3	7
Ministry	1	0	0	1
Editor	1	1	0	2
School teacher	1	0	0	1
Government	0	0	1	1
Artist	0	0	1	1
Total	17	8	9	34
MARITAL STATUS				
Married	15	8	7	30
Divorced	0	0	2	2
Single	2	0	0	2

number of children, being a highly unstable statistic, is not given here. There are many, however. Classification is made within the three major temperamental divisions of the model as of senior year.

Occupations of the members run heavily toward the more traditional professions. Eighteen are now engaged in law, medicine, the ministry, and college teaching. In only two instances is the present occupation inconsistent with the expressed interests and goals of project members at the time of the late senior year standardized interview. Both of these exceptions were instances of a decision to enter medicine after graduation and involved a year or more of post-graduate work to complete medical school prerequisites. Both men are Zs and have great enthusiasm for their choice of medicine as a career. The distribution of the major occupational groups among the varieties of temperament is general. This is in contrast, it will be recalled, to the choice of upper-class major where there was a strong concentration of science and applied social science in the Y group.

Traditionally among growing persons there are two reconstructive stages in life when a major dialogue with oneself is in order. These two periods normally occur in the college years and in the early forties. A meaningful evaluation of college and later development for these thirty-four men should, therefore, await more time. A thorough follow-up study around 1972 would seem a more appropriate time than now. By forty years of age the time will be arriving when the project members, in all likelihood, will be rethinking the wisdom of many of their earlier decisions. By middle age, just as in the college years, old drives will be found wanting and old excuses will have run their course. New well springs, or old ones rediscovered, will found the motive power and new horizons will be due for a view.

Appendix A

Illustrative Interviews

The following seven interviews are presented for illustrative purposes. Four were recorded early in freshman year and three were final senior year interviews. The writer has taken the liberty of editing and deleting many portions of the interviews for the sake of clarity and brevity.

Since all Advisee Project interviews were recorded with the understanding that they would be kept confidential, the three students represented here were recently given an opportunity to delete any statements which they preferred not to make publicly. To see one's interview in print can easily be disconcerting, especially when read many years later. Sensing perhaps the spirit of this endeavor, the persons involved made remarkably few changes in the language and substance of the interview transcriptions.

Inserted between the freshmen and senior interviews is a section of comment entitled, "Clues from the Interview." Placement of a student in the model at a given time was a highly subjective but not arbitrary procedure. The reader is entitled to some clues regarding the procedure used.

Bill—Early Freshman Year [1]
Bill was from eastern Pennsylvania and the son of a clergyman. He had gone to prep school not far from Princeton.

1. Bill's death at the close of his freshman year was a tragic loss to us all. Appreciation is expressed to his family for granting permission to publish excerpts from his early freshman year interview.

During his three years there he was a scholarship student and was graduated top man in his class.

INTERVIEWER: Bill, since this is the first time we have had to record your impression of your life here to date, I wonder if you would start at the beginning and tell me about your initial reactions to Princeton and then follow with your thoughts on Orientation Week and your classes.

BILL: I was very surprised at how much Princeton was as I had expected it and as I had noticed it in the summertime. (He had spent a few days at Princeton in August, buying his furniture from the student-operated furniture exchange.) The only thing that was different was the rain which lasted about three days. It had been nice and sunny here before.

One thing I had noticed in the summer was the real friendliness of everybody I've come in contact with. Beginning with the men selling furniture, from, I mean, the Student Furniture Exchange; this friendliness was carried on in my first day and all. And so far it's been this way in the two weeks I've been at Princeton. I had to get here a day early in order to attend a meeting in the dining hall for those who were to wait on tables there, and I was again struck by the friendliness and the helpfulness of the upperclassmen, and even how friendly the freshmen were.

On looking at the schedules for Orientation Week in the freshman handbook before I came here, I imagined myself having a whole week's time on my hands with practically nothing to do except perhaps an hour a day, but as soon as things started going here, I saw my impression was wrong. I thought that the meetings were very well handled and I was especially impressed by the talks given by upperclassmen about the religious activities, the extra-curricular activities, and the Honor System. I was particularly impressed by a football player giving a talk on the Honor System.

INTERVIEWER: I am glad to hear that everything went so well. How are you getting along with the other fellows here?

BILL: As far as my relations with other people go, naturally I came in contact with my roommates. I had known them very well in school last year and I've continued to get along with them very well. I don't think we've had any major quarrels yet.

INTERVIEWER: Where are you living on the campus, Bill?

BILL: I'm living in Patton Hall, which has really very few freshmen in it, and as a result I'm not really coming in contact with freshmen too intimately except, well, in places like in the dining hall and classes, but as far as knowing freshmen in the dormitories goes, there's only one in our entryway and as a result I really haven't come to know any freshmen as well as I knew people at school at this time last year. All four of us in the room have become very friendly with the two juniors and a sophomore who are living across the hall. The sophomore is really very nice; the juniors, I'm not quite sure about them— they seem to, well, I don't know exactly how to express it, they seem to—I suppose they're sort of a type that one expects to see in college.

INTERVIEWER: What type do you mean?

BILL: You know, the type that invariably goes to bed with two bottles of beer which they keep in somebody else's refrigerator. I haven't noticed their applying themselves too industriously to their studies. They just seem to be the type who know their way around New York, or at least give you the impression that they do.

INTERVIEWER: Do you think they are like the average student here?

BILL: No, I wouldn't say that they are the average, but they're sort of what you'd think of as typical.

INTERVIEWER: The typical Charlie, you mean?

BILL: Yes, that's it, that's it exactly. I'd say for the most part the students I have come in contact with wouldn't be put in the Charlie class. Most of them seem to be pretty serious about their studies and work pretty hard. It might be that the Charlie group is just more in evidence. You don't notice a person that goes around with his head down and carrying his books.

INTERVIEWER: Do you like your courses, Bill?

BILL: One of the courses I'm most pleased with so far is my English course. This is primarily because it's changed from a class into a precept (round-table discussion group). I think I'll get much more out of it. I like very much the way that each student is on his own in reading the plays; we're not led through it in class. Each student is left to his own devices and can get just as much out of each play as he likes. The lecturer, Professor Stauffer, is one of the best I've ever heard. He certainly is the best lecturer that I have right now in college. He manages to keep his lectures interesting and packs just as much information in them as I think is possible. All in all I'm very much pleased with that course. I like the professor I have in precept, also. That's Mr. Riggs. I was somewhat disturbed by his chain smoking at first, but I've gotten used to that and I'm getting a lot out of his sessions.

Originally the class periods were scheduled with two different one-hour periods in the morning, but it has been changed now into a two-hour precept in the evening with informal discussions around a table. It's really made it a lot better; just the atmosphere while sitting around the table as equals, instead of sitting back in your chair and listening to the professor futilely trying to get the conversation going.

INTERVIEWER: What about your other courses?

BILL: I was expecting my German to be rather hard,

since I was put ahead one term, but so far I've found it to be very easy and I'll probably spend less time on that course than any of my others. I think that more could be gotten out of the course somehow. We do a few pages of reading at night and then in class we merely translate that into English. I think that if the student could be allowed on his own more, so that he wouldn't have to be checked up on his reading in class, we'd get a lot more out of the course. I'd suggest that we have more conversation in German class. I expected the course to be done entirely in that and so far English certainly predominates in the class-room.

Politics is a course I'm getting to like very much despite the lecturer and my teacher. It can be a rather dry course, I think, and the professors almost seem to do their best to make it that way. At least, the ones I've experienced. But the material that we cover is very interesting and I enjoy especially the outside reading that we do from the books in the library.

My music course is elementary harmony and is about what I expected it to be. Mr. Cone is the lecturer and I have Mr. Keppler in precept. The room that we have the lecture in is just about the dingiest room imaginable; it has a large, bleak aspect—it lends a dampening aspect to the course, somehow. Of course, that shouldn't be very important but it just seems that way to me. I've had piano before but it hasn't been too difficult for me so far. I'm being checked up on a lot of things I missed and I think I'm really going to get a lot of value out of the course.

Physics is by far the most difficult of the courses I'm taking. I've never been very good in math, but I have been good in memorization. I was somewhat disconcerted to find that the course required a lot more mathematics and a lot less memorization than I expected. It's presented in a

THE REASONABLE ADVENTURER

very interesting way, primarily because, through the efforts of Professor Rogers, there's always something going on in the lecture, some explosion or well-set-up experiment. I was really amazed at the intricacy of some of these experiments. It must have taken hours to set up some of those experiments.

INTERVIEWER: Not being out for a freshman team, you have to take physical education, do you not?

BILL: Yes, that's right, sir, but I like it a lot. I expected to be least pleased with physical education, but I like it a lot. I had wanted to take tennis instruction in the beginning, but couldn't get into that group, so I'm now in soccer. I had never played any soccer before and I was glad to find that the instruction is based on the assumption that those who are taking soccer know nothing about it. And as a result I've learned the fundamentals of soccer and am really getting a lot of enjoyment. The hours for soccer are scheduled in the morning and therefore it doesn't break up the afternoon as much. Also, it doesn't make you quite so sleepy by the time your 11:40 class comes along. As you know, I was never too interested in sports at school. I liked to play on my own, but as far as organized sports goes, I wasn't too interested in it, but now I'm finding that I really like playing soccer.

INTERVIEWER: We had better stop here, Bill, as it is 10:30. Thanks a lot for coming in.

BILL: Not at all, sir. I hope I have given you what you need for our project. I have really enjoyed talking with you. After the first few minutes one forgets all about the fact that what they are saying is actually being recorded.

INTERVIEWER: Yes, I think having a small microphone attached to your lapel is better than trying to talk into some microphone set before you.

BILL: I believe you're right. I'll see you, sir.

Bob—Early Freshman Year

The time had come for Bob's first regularly scheduled conference with me, with many other sessions to come. From my visit to his home in August, I knew him as a product of a midwest high school. Even though Bob's family could have afforded it, I doubt very much if they ever seriously considered sending him to an eastern prep school.

INTERVIEWER: How do you like it here, Bob?

BOB: Very much, my reaction on the whole is really good. The first thing I noticed when I got on this campus was how nicely the upperclassmen received you and went out of their way to help the freshmen all they could. I didn't expect them to be unfriendly, of course, but I never realized how interested they all would be in making us feel right at home.

Did you see the rally Saturday night?

INTERVIEWER: You mean the freshman class rally in Alexander Hall?

BOB: Yes. That was really wonderful. The true Princeton spirit certainly entered the minds of the freshmen even though we have only been here a week. I can see our class going right into line with every other preceding class as far as spirit and all that goes. They had the band there; we cheered. It was really great!

INTERVIEWER: How's the football going?

BOB: I had to drop football. I began to worry whether I could carry my studies. In fact, I phoned my father about it. He said I should talk it over with you and do what I thought best. I knew mother would be just as happy if I did quit football but Dad got his letter in football at Ohio State. Our coach was certainly as nice as anybody could be to a fellow that had to make a decision. He appreciated my coming to talk with him about it. It was not the physical exertion during practice that got me but more that I got too tired to study at night. I made my decision to quit on Wednesday and all day Thursday I just wondered. I started talking to the guys and they said, "Are you gonna quit?" They said I was silly to quit because I had a chance to make the team.

INTERVIEWER: Have you definitely decided?

BOB: Yes, I just can't do it. I can't play football and carry my studies and I feel my studies are more important, at least for the first semester.

INTERVIEWER: What do you think of your classmates, Bob?

BOB: As far as the fellows in my dorm, there's a fellow from Charleston, West Virginia, and one from Columbus, Ohio, and another from Brazil. They're all freshmen; they come to our room and we have big bull sessions at night. They're really right guys, if you know what I mean. Underneath they're the same kind of guys as in our room. I'm sure the same situation prevails in every other dorm. I know that the Class of 1954 is really going to be united as far as friendly relationships are concerned.

INTERVIEWER: And your roommates?

BOB: Oh, my roommates are swell. I know one boy very well as he lives in my home town and he brought the other fellow from the prep school that he went to. So the three of us are together and they're tops, they really are. The way the fellows that go to school here dress is something I wasn't quite expecting. I thought it would be just a little bit more formal. I know you told me at home this summer that it was not going to be, but you know you expect to see just a little more formal clothing. Not that I don't like it because I like to be as informal as I possibly can too, but you see fellows around the dorm in blue jeans and T shirts and old moldy tennis shoes. I think in a way it helps because it makes school informal just like it always has been, at least where I came from. These past two nights we've been having fights with the sophomores and everybody's been coming in looking pretty ragged; everybody's perspiring like mad, their shirts all torn and everything like that. It's kind of a sad sight but it's great!

(Bob came back the next week for his second interview. The day before the interview I had noticed him watching the freshman-sophomore softball game.)

INTERVIEWER: What did you think of the softball game yesterday, Bob?

BOB: I'm sure glad we won. That Whitehouse fellow really did a great job of pitching. He was the whole team practically. I didn't get a chance to see the ending because I had to go back to the room and study a little before dinner. I found out after dinner that we had won. That was terrific!

INTERVIEWER: Oh, it's too bad you missed the ending.

BOB: Yes, but I did have to get back. I had to type up a politics theme. I have to go to New York with my folks over the weekend so I have to get part of next week's assignment done.

INTERVIEWER: I was glad to see your mother and father this morning, Bob. I almost didn't recognize them at first.

BOB: They were very happy to have the opportunity to talk with you.

INTERVIEWER: They seemed pretty pleased at the way things are going for you.

BOB: I think they are. I don't know. It seems to me they are. They're crazy about this place. They're really bowled over. I took Dad to see the library and the chapel. That sold him! I had some reservations for them at the Tavern and they were talking to some people who have a boy up here and they said the Inn was better.

INTERVIEWER: Do you think you are keeping caught up on your work?

BOB: Yes, although I'm a little bit behind in politics

and naval science. As far as the reading goes, I mean, there's no real trouble. I passed a math test the other day; I consider that a real accomplishment. The only subject that really worries me is math. This math teacher, he's very unusual. He still hasn't told us his name, incidentally. He knows his stuff, but it's a question of trying to get it across to us. Gee, he got off something this morning that just completely lost about three-quarters of us. Something about adding complex roots and we're not even near that. It's kinda hard.

INTERVIEWER: I told your father, Bob, that I'd talk to you about your math. That was one of the things he asked me about. My suggestion is that you try one or two things; first, that you go to the instructor and tell him what you don't understand. You won't be asking for anything beyond the call of duty. That's part of his job. If I were you, I'd just drop by his office and ask him when you could see him in regard to going over your difficulties.

BOB: Well, I'll see how it goes. This passing of this test encouraged me, it gave me a new light on the situation. I don't know, if things get too much over my head, why I'll go to him and ask him to help if he can.

INTERVIEWER: Did you go to the football game last Saturday?

BOB: The Navy game? Oh that was terrific. As a matter of fact that's the first game where I have *really* gotten into the spirit of yelling. It's the first time I guess our team had to put out. It was a fine game. One thing that I was wondering about, though. On those big weekends there isn't anything for the freshmen to do. Well, say, your date comes Friday night, there's not much of a problem because of the pep rally and all that. But Saturday, after the game you're allowed in the dorm until seven, beyond which time no women are allowed inside. Then there's a dance at nine. That's—ah—because you eat between seven and nine, and after the dance folds up at twelve there is no place to go.

INTERVIEWER: In other words you still felt like going somewhere?

BOB: Yes, you know. I guess a lot of kids go down to the lake, and you can get kinda cold down there.

INTERVIEWER: It's quite a walk too.

BOB: You bet it's quite a walk. I don't know whether there is any place designated for freshmen to go.

INTERVIEWER: That's probably true, Bob, unless, of course, you want to go into town to get something to eat again.

BOB: That gets to be a financial problem then. There's no place that's inside, see?

INTERVIEWER: That is a problem I guess.

BOB: Well, I didn't know whether anybody else felt the same way or not, but, you know, I thought I'd bring it up. . . . What else have I to tell you? I don't know, I guess everything's going along fine.

INTERVIEWER: What about the future?

BOB: What about it?

INTERVIEWER: Oh, I was just wondering what you might want to major in your upperclass years. Have you given it any thought?

BOB: As a matter of fact, I have; I think I'm going to major in religion, as it seems now. A lot depends on how the religion course goes next term. It looks pretty interesting.

INTERVIEWER: Does that mean you are again thinking seriously of going into the ministry?

BOB: Yes, I'd say it was very prominent in my mind right now.

INTERVIEWER: Fine, let's talk about it next time.

Michael—Early Freshman Year
Michael came from a small town just below the Mason and Dixon Line. He was the first student from his high

school ever to come to Princeton. The principal had felt that Michael was a very promising young man and had suggested his name to Princeton's director of admissions. Coming to college was a whole new world for Michael. At first I thought it would be some time before he would warm up to our relationship, but I was wrong.

INTERVIEWER: Well, Michael, what were your impressions of the orientation meeting, the first class meeting you went to?

MICHAEL: I was glad to see the men but that's about all. The first couple of days we were really scared. There were eight boys at my end of the hall and seven of the eight were ready to pack up and go home if they could. The other one, the only reason he didn't want to was because his mother and father were still staying in Princeton. He was seeing them every day and going places with them.

INTERVIEWER: What was the trouble?

MICHAEL: Well, we were worried that we wouldn't be able to keep up with our lessons, that we would flunk out and have to go back home. That is the biggest disgrace in the world, just about. The other night a senior came down to the room next to ours to see a boy he knew. After he got there he stayed for two or three hours and all the freshmen came around and we had quite a bull session and he really gave us the lowdown on the school. He made us feel a lot better because we were really worried and really scared. I understand that the Orange Key [a student organization] is supposed to send somebody around, but they should have come around sooner, like within the first three days after you arrive and really talk to you. The way he did it was good. I think you get more out of it if it is a larger group than just the ones in your room, and yet not too large a group. The group was perfect. There was about a maximum of twelve and there were never less than eight and we just kept a good conversation going all the time.

INTERVIEWER: It was the academic aspect that really worried them, that was what made them think they wanted to go home?

MICHAEL: Yes, *sir*.

INTERVIEWER: I mean they liked the other parts of Princeton?

MICHAEL: Oh, yes, sir. It was just worry about lessons. I want to drop French 101!

INTERVIEWER: What for?

MICHAEL: I don't know, it's just—it requires so much time that I don't have time to do my other lessons. I think my other subjects are going to suffer because of French. In other words, to do that good I would have to devote much more time to it than to any other subject and the other ones would suffer. Actually, the only reason I took it was because I wanted to just pick up some French. I'm not really interested in it, although I am interested in my politics and my history and my English. I didn't particularly relish my English at first, but after I got in class and listened to the instructor, I like it now, because we really have a good instructor.

INTERVIEWER: Who is your instructor?

MICHAEL: Mr. Ludwig. He really paints pictures of Shakespeare. I never really studied Shakespeare's lines before too carefully when I was in high school. As I remember, the first day I took it here I was talking to one of my roommates about it and he really liked Shakespeare and I said, "Well, I don't know yet," I wasn't crazy about him. But now I am, you begin to look for things much more than you did in high school. My roommates and I went home last weekend. We left here Saturday and came back Sunday. But I'm glad we went, now, because it took some of the restlessness out of us. And in our corner in the dorm most of the boys are from high school. The ones in the room right next to us. We all get together and start talking and you find that everybody that came from a high school really liked his high school, and so far aren't particularly crazy about Princeton. That's the truth about everybody that came from high school, unless they lived in this vicinity. But everybody that comes from a prep school is crazy about Princeton in contrast to the prep school. When you come here from high school, I think there is a big difference, especially right now.

INTERVIEWER: What is the difference, do you think?

MICHAEL: The boys aren't prepared, for one thing, but I think that within a couple of years we will be even ahead of them. Well, I don't know—I wouldn't want a boy to go to a prep school for anything. If I have a son, he is going to a public school and if he doesn't have good enough grades to go to college he will go to a prep school for a year after he graduates from public school. But he is going to go to public school. I think if you miss high school you miss out on a lot of things. These boys that go to prep school, they've been more or less shut away from everything and I think they really miss out on a lot of fun. Of course, when you talk to them, their attitude is just the opposite, I mean, they really like it. They've lived in an environment of this type and we haven't. Now, I want to drop French because . . . .

(So I went over Michael's College Board test scores with him. He could see then that, except for one subject, advanced math, he was well above the average for Princeton on all of his College Boards; and the advanced math wasn't too far below the average for Princeton, at that. This seemed to make him feel more confident that he really could compete with the rest of the students here. He talked a good deal about his pride in his work and participation in the Student Council, in basketball, and in other special activities at his home town high school.)

MICHAEL: At least I don't feel so discouraged about

Princeton. . . . I was really disliking the place when I came in to see you this morning.

INTERVIEWER: How are things going?

MICHAEL: Yesterday I accomplished the most since I've come to this University as far as work goes. I was way behind and I was determined to get something done. I'm still behind. I failed a music test the other day. I don't understand what's going on in music at all.

Marks are worrying me. If I could come out at midterms with a third group average (rough equivalent of a C average) or somewhere around there, I'd feel a lot better. I'd stop worrying. I'd enjoy it here much more then. If I came out at mid-terms with a third average, a third group, then I'd be able to. I wouldn't have to work every night like I'm doing now. I'd be able to play basketball in the afternoon and do that conditioning like I was telling you about, and I'd enjoy it much more, I'm pretty sure. When you worry, you must worry and worry all the time. One thing, I'm going to try and get more sleep and everything and plan things out better and go to bed earlier because by the time ten o'clock or ten-thirty comes I've used up my capacity to study, anyhow, and the reading I do after that is negligible. I mean, I read it but I don't understand what I am reading, so I may as well go to bed.

INTERVIEWER: You really feel tired?

MICHAEL: Well, I don't know. I don't feel tired. I could sit and talk in the room for a couple of hours, but I just lose my power to concentrate. That's the biggest trouble —if I get something done, it's at that moment I have the power to concentrate; if I don't, it's because at that moment I lose it. I can't figure out why it is sometimes I can and sometimes I can't.

INTERVIEWER: You *are* getting out from under, aren't you?

MICHAEL: Yes, a little. I am beginning to learn how to

use my time. I don't waste so much time any more, like when they start shooting the bull in the room I get up and leave and go in and study. There's a boy next door to us, a nice guy, but he studies—if he doesn't get a second group, he ought to be shot, the way he studies! Oh, no kidding, all the time he just studies, and he's not taking really tough courses.

I really like every one of my subjects now except music. Every one of them I understand what's going on. It's just that I have to do some additional reading and additional work to get caught up to where we should be, but—

INTERVIEWER: That's true of the math too?

MICHAEL: Yes, so far. I have right much to do, though, for Thursday. Today I am going to do my history and politics and get that out of the way. I've done my English for this week. English I do pretty well, I mean, I do it pretty far ahead of time. Like I did last Friday, I think, this week's English. I hope he likes my theme. I wrote on . . . the love in *Romeo and Juliet,* and the way it affects me is what it amounts to.

INTERVIEWER: Tell me about it.

MICHAEL: I forgot what—oh, "Shakespeare's Use of Human Emotions" is my title. It's not a good title. I had to have a title. I just took the play, I took each love scene like, for each idea of love that was in it, and tried to bring out how he used this play on our emotions. In other words, by doing it in such a way, it affected us in such a way. In other words, it brought out pity in us; it brought out sorrow; it brought happiness and things like that in a person reading a play. Basically, it's just, it just has one idea in it; it's not full of ideas. Like some themes, I know my roommate's first themes were character sketches. They were full of ideas. Mine is all one idea just about. In some parts the wording is good, I think, I feel it is, because I— well, I don't—there's one boy next door, he's a nice guy too, but he wants to use big words, so to do it he sits there and he thinks of what he wants to say and then he looks up in a synonym dictionary for a big word for the word he's going to use. Well, I can't see that. I don't do that. I just write and if I know a big word or if the words come, I just write what comes naturally. And when I reread it I try to make words fit, like a certain adjective will fit a certain noun much better than another one will. I try to make sure that I have the right one and cross out the one I don't have. But I think the sentence and wording is pretty good. I thought it was fair. I thought it was pretty fair when I'd written it. I let my roommates read it and their criticism was, "What are you getting at?" In other words, it was just a plot, what happened in a plot, what happened to the people? Well, they differ from me in the fact that I think it's important how it affects people. In other words, I don't think that the mechanics of the plot make much difference; how he brought this in or that. But I think the fact that because he had this there it affected the person that read it in this way, and that's where your enjoyment of it comes from. Like I enjoyed Romeo, they say *Romeo and Juliet* isn't one of his best plays. But I enjoyed it as much as any play I've ever read by him just because I became interwoven with the story; just lost myself in it. And every time something happened to Romeo, I felt bad about it too.

Don—Early Freshman Year
Don was from southern California and he had attended a prep school there. His mother and father were born and educated in the East but had moved to California when he was quite young. At heart Don was all Californian, sometimes belligerently so. When he came to Princeton, all easterners were suspect. In spite of this, he came East to college

because it was here that he felt he could get the most thorough liberal arts education. He was well into his upperclass years before I ever saw him wear a white oxford shirt with a button-down collar; he kept to his western shirts with the open collar. As he moved about the campus he presented a defiant contrast to the eastern lads clad in white shirts, khaki pants, athletic socks, and dirty white buck shoes.

INTERVIEWER: This is your first week of classes, Don, but let's go back one week and talk about your thoughts and feelings as you arrived on the scene here.

DON: My first reaction as I came into Princeton was that one has to look out for himself. If I weren't to be fairly careful and hold on to my wallet, I'd soon find that I would spend a lot of money for unnecessary things. A newly arrived student has to understand that he is on his own from the very beginning. For example, as I stepped off the train and collected my baggage I either could have taken a taxi and been taken exactly where I was to go, started walking, or I could have looked around for someone to tell me how to get there. Rather than spend an exorbitant price on a taxi I waited around and soon found that one of the students driving a furniture exchange truck would take me right to my room. As I went to my room I noticed that no one was much interested in what was going on as far as I was concerned, but that each person must work out what he wants to do for himself and do it. No one is going to tell you in college just what you have to do and it is up to you to do what you think is worthwhile.

INTERVIEWER: Is that pretty much what you expected or did you think the first week would turn out different than that?

DON: That was pretty much what I expected . . . yes, although I thought that possibly the people I had known before might not be so occupied with what they were doing themselves.

INTERVIEWER: Isn't there some way in which college so far has turned out differently?

DON: No, I felt that college would be pretty much this way . . . this way meaning that one has to work out things for himself and judge what is important by himself, that one would have to study at his own leisure. And I felt that the first week was rather poor in one way in that there were not enough things that ought to be done. There was too much time that one could just loaf or get oriented in the town. The orientation is a necessary thing, but when there is so much extra time at first it makes the student feel that possibly he won't have so much to do and he will be able to spend all his time loafing.

INTERVIEWER: You feel that there was time that could have been used to better advantage. What is your impression of the Class of 1954?

DON: My impression now is that it takes time to understand each individual, and that these first impressions are rather poor. I found that at first my impressions were that the majority hadn't really come here for an education, but now I am finding more and more that do seem the right sort of men and probably will get a great deal out of it.

I need to get a job as soon as I can, and I want to get down and get most of my studies started as well as I can.

INTERVIEWER: When you were admitted what did the Bureau of Student Aid promise you in the way of a part-time job?

DON: They had given me a scholarship and a loan but they did not promise any job. I was told to come in when I got to college; I talked with Mr. Morgan and he said to come in at a later date.

INTERVIEWER: You really want to work?

DON: Yes, I do.

INTERVIEWER: What sort of work would you like to do?

DON: Oh, anything is fine by me. I would like to work in the laboratories if there is any available work because I am interested in scientific studies. Or I would just as soon wait tables in the dining halls.

INTERVIEWER: Are there any other comments you would like to make, Don, about the first two weeks of college?

DON: I found that ideas spread very rapidly throughout the campus. For instance, in our Freshman Week we were not told anything as to what books we should buy and when we should buy them as far as I know. But within the first two days just about every freshman knew he had to buy his own books before classes and knew how to find out which books he needed. Also, I found that the class spirit was greatly strengthened by things which rose from individuals in the class. For instance, in our Freshman Rally Saturday night, two boys from the South got up and played some hillbilly songs, and that tied the class together a lot more than the cheers which were led by upperclassmen. As far as I can see, the most necessary thing that a freshman in college must do is figure out what things he places value on and set aside time for those things and make sure that he puts in plenty of time on his studies if he values them or extracurricular activities or whatever he does value, and not waste his time in bull sessions because there is always something going on on the campus. One could waste all of his time by not deciding what is important.

INTERVIEWER: Fine. Now would you tell me something about your courses and how you think you will do in them?

DON: As to my courses I was told before I came to Princeton by a member of the sophomore class of two courses that I really ought to try and get into—one was the honors course in math taught by Professor Artin, whom I was told was one of the best in the country.

Another course I was told I ought to get into was the honors section in chemistry. I was somewhat disappointed in not getting into that, but having gotten into the regular section I find it an excellent course with a top-notch instructor. Professor Turkevich seems to be a person who is full of life and quite human. He explains his course very well and puts a lot of life into it to make it something that a person would want to do.

As for history, it is a very interesting course, but one that is quite difficult because of the great amount of reading that must be done. Now as to how I will come out in these courses:

In math it's rather hard to tell because so far it's hard to understand the instructor to a certain extent, and it's hard to know just how much I've grasped. But I imagine if I work hard I'll come out fairly well.

As to chemistry, a certain amount of review is necessary but with a lot more life and interest in it, so I should do all right in chemistry.

English seems to be an interesting course, as well as the regular lectures and Shakespeare. It's hard to tell just how I'll do, but the instructor seems to be very good.

As for German, up to now there's been very simple work, but today, for the first time, the course got rough, so maybe German will be a difficult language, although at the start it seemed easy, but with a thorough amount of effort it seems that with the good instruction and frequent drill, I should be able to come out all right.

History, it's hard to estimate because I did poorly in history at school and I find it easier here to tie things together, only being held for basic trends rather than all the little details.

INTERVIEWER: And your plan of study . . . ?

DON: As to my plan of study, I find the most satisfactory thing is to read over my week's assignment in history, English, chemistry, and get those three out of the way and take a certain amount of notes on the reading assignment and then more notes in class. Then at the end of the week summarize both the class notes and the notes from the reading of the previous week. Finally, study those notes which indicate the basic trends, for example, the main outline of the play in English or the main ideas of the chapters in chemistry.

In German and math, we get weekly assignments rather than assignments for the whole term, so I more or less do those as they come and try to prepare for those just before each class.

INTERVIEWER: Before you go, Don, I would like to hear a little more about what impressions your classmates have made on you.

DON: My reactions to the people here at college are quite varied. It's hard to group them into one type, they're extremely different. I feel it would be easy to make friends in the sense that there are plenty of people of every type and description. But it will be hard in the sense that it will take time to meet the people and get to know them better.

INTERVIEWER: Yes, I see what you mean.

DON: I started out rooming with boys I'd already known, and so I have a fairly satisfactory arrangement. However, outside of these, even though I run around with a group of five or six, I haven't really found people of the same sort of temperament as I am. I've found, on the whole, that the majority of the student body is quite friendly and willing to help in every sort of way.

INTERVIEWER: Where were you during the (freshman-sophomore) riots?

DON: I was there. The classes showed a lot of spirit.

They fought hard, but whenever anyone went down they stopped and helped the guy up so he wouldn't be hurt badly. I participated in all the main riots in Holder Court and in front of Commons and in the big riot out in front of Nassau Hall, but missed the riot the other night after the rally. The class rivalry seems to be rather a stupid thing, but it's sure a hell of a lot of fun.

Clues from the Interviews

It may now be of interest to the reader to see how the model was applied using clues from the interview transcripts. To this end the early freshman year interviews of the four students will be reviewed. The freshman year model positions of Bill, Bob, Michael, and Don are indicated in Figure 18.

As will be seen, the early interviews provided relatively more clues for judging positions on the XYZ dimension than for rating the distance of each student from point A. As a matter of fact the developmental dimension ratings were generally found to be more difficult to make than were the dimensions of temperament. Statements from the early freshman year interviews extracted for the present discussion are found within quotation marks. Key phrases are in italics. As before, we begin with Bill.

BILL: 1. "One thing I had noticed in the summer was the *real friendliness* of everybody. . . . this *friendliness* was carried on in my first day and all. And so far it's been this way in the two weeks I've been at Princeton. . . . I was again struck by *the friendliness and the helpfulness* of the upperclassmen and even how *friendly* the freshmen were."

This emphasis on reception is suggestive for placement on the X side of the model.

2. "I've continued to get along with them (roommates) very well. I don't think we've had any major quarrels yet."

FIGURE 18.

Freshman Year Positions of Four Students

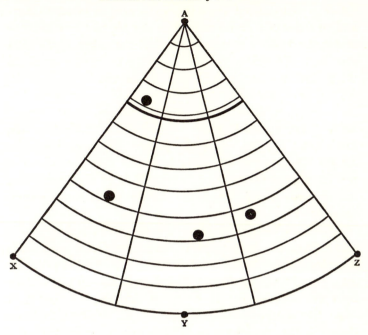

An X's concern for keeping the peace?

3. Bill's comments on his courses suggest genuine satisfaction. Also he likes the opportunity to work at his own pace. He is self-propelling in his academic life and apparently likes to be challenged. He is discovering a new satisfaction in physical education. This is early evidence (later confirmed) that Bill is closer to the A point in the model than to the X point.

BOB: 1. "The first thing I noticed when I got on this campus was how nicely the upperclassmen *received you* and went out of their way *to help* the freshman all they could. . . . I never realized how interested they all would be in *making us feel right at home*."

Reveals X's concern to be accepted by the group. Perhaps had some earlier anxiety regarding acceptance by the group.

2. "The *true Princeton spirit* certainly entered the minds of *the* freshman. . . . I can see *our* class going right into line with every other preceding class."

Note ready identification with class as well as a perception of the class as part of an even larger body, Princeton through the ages, etc. Sees oneself already incorporated in the group. He belongs!

3. "I had to drop football."

The interviewer had to raise this problem. A Z would have introduced a worry more readily. (Some may think that Bob's taking the matter up with his mother, father, coach, and fellow students is indicative of an X's dependence on external direction. This decision, I believe, Bob made quite on his own. The consultation with relevant parties was to my thinking more of a sounding out to find what repercussions might occur should he quit—not an unreasonable move.)

4. "As far as the fellows in my dorm (are concerned), . . . *Underneath* they're the *same kind of guys* as in our room. I'm sure the *same situation prevails* in every other dorm . . . . the class of 1954 is really going to be *united* as far as *friendly* relationships are concerned."

More evidence of striving for identification with group and dedifferentiation. Differences are not real differences; underneath "we are one and together."

5. Note so far in the interview that it was structured by the interviewer. The Z classification can be ruled out in this case.

6. "Well, I'll see how it goes. This passing of this (math) test encouraged me."

A Y would not be content with the mere passing of a test. (Note too that Bob did not commit himself to getting help from his instructor as I advised. Going to see the instructor might be threatening in itself. Incidentally, Bob's cautiousness never appeared to extend to the physical realm. I was later to see him on the varsity baseball team make plays with seemingly utter disregard for his personal safety.)

7. "What else have I to tell you? . . . *I guess everything's going along fine.*"

8. "I think I'm going to major in religion."

A Y would have introduced such a plan without specific inquiry. Also a Y would have welcomed a chance to elaborate on his vocational aims.

The reader may agree with an X classification for Bob but ask why I placed him slightly toward Y. If one were to listen to this interview, he would detect greater assertiveness and emphasis in speech than is possible from the written transcript. Another Y'ish feature is that Bob's conscience is more effective than one would expect, as evidenced by his leaving the softball game early to return to his studies. For most Xs morality begins when someone is heard at the door. Also, would not one expect most ministers to be an XY rather than a straight X or Y?

MICHAEL: 1. "I was glad to see the men but that's about all. The first couple of days we were really scared."

Devotes only one sentence to the inquiry regarding reactions to the first orientation meeting. Quickly moves to a matter of more personal concern. This pattern of the interviewee's controlling the course of the interview persists. The control does not seem to be consciously done but more through rolling along a chain of internally linked ideas, in true Z fashion.

2. Note the preference throughout for subjectivity. His English theme, characteristically, was on Shakespeare's ability to elicit *feeling* in the reader.

3. The first interview was two hours in length, a fact

almost sufficient to justify a Z classification. In the early stages of the project at least, it would have been unusual for an X or Y to take that much time. Michael was "wound up." When this is the case the Z seemingly has no alternative but to unwind.

4. Michael's identification with a group, albeit an "out group," caused me to move him toward the YZ somewhat. He would be no mere follower in this group, however. Identifications of the Y are generally with a special group rather than with the group as a whole. A far right Z will join a far left X and watch the world go by. A Y'ish Z is more eager to get into the stream.

5. Unless he's in a state of apathy, the Z is easy to spot by his lack of organization and ready flow of thoughts and feelings. Michael is no exception. Note the gain in control, however, in his final senior year interview.

DON: 1. The fact that Don apparently never wore a button-down collar until he was well into his upperclass years seems to indicate that he was a Y or, perhaps, a Z, but hardly an X.

2. "My first reaction as I came into Princeton was that one has to look out for himself."

". . . I noticed that no one was much interested in what was going on as far as I was concerned. . . ."

Note the contrast with Bob's ready identification with the group in general. Don clearly is differentiating himself from the group, at least initially. The Y is generally not as trusting as either the X or the Z. He seems to say to himself, "This looks like a good guy *but* maybe first appearances are deceiving."

3. ". . . each person must work out what he wants to do for himself and do it . . . it is up to you to do what you think is worthwhile."

The reader will note throughout statements like the above which will remind him of the "Protestant Ethic" as described by W. H. Whyte, Jr., in *The Organization Man.* Don at this stage is a "hard guy." Compare this typical lower Y outlook, however, with the content of Don's final senior year interview.

4. ". . . there were not enough things that ought to be done . . . there is so much *extra time* at first it makes the student feel that . . . he will be able to spend all his time *loafing.*"

". . . a freshman in college must . . . not *waste his time* in bull sessions. . . ."

Waste of anything is, of course, a cardinal sin for the Y.

5. ". . . one was the *honors* course in math taught by Professor Artin, whom I was told was *one of the best* in the country. . . . I . . . [felt that I should] get into the *honors section* in chemistry . . . [but the regular section turned out to be] "an *excellent* course with a *top notch* instructor."

A Y's concern for obtaining for himself the very best.

6. ". . . but with a thorough amount of effort . . . and frequent drill, I should be able to come out all right."

A Y's capacity for and faith in plain hard work.

7. "As to my plan of study . . . at the end of the week [I] summarize both the class notes and the notes from the reading of the previous week."

A well-organized study schedule. The Y characteristically plans ahead and, what's more, often adheres to it. Don was a prodigious worker.

8. "It's hard to group them [classmates] into one type. . . ."

The Y distrusts generalization. This is allied to my comment on note 2 for Don.

9. Finally, note that this interview is of the prepared statement type. Its good organization reflects not only anticipation of my questions but also a thorough mulling over prior to the interview.

This concludes our review of four students' early freshman year interviews for clues in regard to placement in the personality model. As can be noted in the final senior interview of three of these men, there was considerable development to come.

Bill's death was one of two in the Advisee Project during my four years with these men. Tragedies such as these are difficult to bear. Bill was one of the most lovable and promising members of the Advisee Project, one of the charter members in our group of Reasonable Adventurers.

Bob—Late Senior Year

Six hundred college careers at Princeton were rapidly coming to an end. Like any other process of coming down to the wire, it was a hectic period, full of implementing plans for the future even though the big test—final comprehensive examinations—lay directly ahead. Finding a two or three hour spot for the final senior year interview [2] was no easy feat. Once Bob did find time in his busy schedule, he came in for a general review of his four years and a look to the future.

INTERVIEWER: Bob, now that your thesis is over, how do you feel about it?

BOB: Well, it's hard to say. Now that it's over with I don't know as I feel too much differently than when I was preparing it—when I was looking forward to writing it. Naturally, now that it's in, it's a great relief. It's a big weight off my shoulders. But I've always felt the thesis could be the most challenging and yet the most rewarding thing about Princeton—if you really get interested in your

2. The final interview of each semester was "standardized." I had planned a series of topics which the student and I usually followed in sequence. A copy of the topical outline was handed to the student at the beginning of the interview.

topic and attempt to do an adult job on it. I tried as best I could to put the very best of my ability into it and, as a result, now that it is over, I don't look back on it with any particular misgivings. I don't feel any strong urge that I should have done a better job or that I could have done a better job because I don't think I could have. I think only in minor aspects could I have done a better job. I think that I put the very best of myself into it. I feel that it has been an extremely rewarding experience. I don't feel in my mind that I sluffed off any responsibility that I had toward it.

INTERVIEWER: In terms of felt satisfaction, was it an enjoyable experience at any point? If so, at what point?

BOB: It was enjoyable in the writing of it. At certain times I was really putting something down that I felt was a good point. I spent a lot of time trying to develop these points. That happened several times during the process of writing it. I wouldn't say it was extremely enjoyable doing the research on it. A lot of times that was just a procedure you had to go through.

INTERVIEWER: How do you feel about the idea of departmental concentration and a senior thesis as related to your other work?

BOB: I think departmental concentration is very good. I think, however, that to make this place really effective, this business of a thesis should not be caught in the middle —now maybe that's where they want it, and that could well be—but other things demand so much of your time that you are torn between doing a good job on your thesis and letting your work go, or doing more or less of a halfway job on both. I would like to see, and I think it would do more good for the student, to have more weight attached to the thesis and have the students turn out a real scholarly effort to graduate, if they want the thesis at all. I would think that it would be more effective to have electives optional—and have the only thing that is required be a long thesis—by that I mean a minimum of 40,000 words, running anywhere up to 100,000 words. I believe that the thesis is the most important part of your education up here.

INTERVIEWER: Can you say something about your relationship with your thesis supervisor?

BOB: My relationship with my supervisor was excellent. My supervisor was Professor Fine, classics department. He helped me in the beginning with the selection of my topic and helped me all the way through. Also, he was willing and able to see me almost at any time. He read everything that I wrote before I rewrote it, and he gave me a lot of very good suggestions, allowing me to do with them what I wished, to incorporate them or not. He was really superb, I felt.

INTERVIEWER: Good. Looking back over your four years here, what have been the major sources of deep satisfaction that you think have favorably influenced your development?

BOB: Well, the intellectual atmosphere in general; although many times I get quite provoked at it. I think down deep when I will be able to sit back and look at it, I think that living in this type of atmosphere for four years did me a lot of good. I think the people that I met have probably been the greatest source of satisfaction—learning to appreciate. . . .

INTERVIEWER: You mean the students?

BOB: Yes. Learning to appreciate the worth of people with whom I did not necessarily have anything in common.

INTERVIEWER: Now, what do you think has been the net change in your intellectual life between freshman year and now?

BOB: Probably the biggest change that has come about in my intellectual life has been a desire to read, not anything in particular, but everything in general. I will find a satisfaction in reading which I never had before.

INTERVIEWER: Very good. What would you say was the net change in your relations with peers—that is, people your own age and sex? Considering how your personal relationships were in your freshman year and what they seem to be now, is there any net change?

BOB: I don't believe there is any net change. I don't think I have developed in this respect. That is the one thing that is probably the biggest thing that has disturbed me about Princeton. I don't think my relationships with my fellow people have changed. I mean, my outlook toward them might have changed but my relationships with them have not changed. I think it's about the same. I wish it were better. I will say, however, that I feel I had an extremely fortunate background before I came here with my fellow people.

INTERVIEWER: How about your relationship with girls? Is there any change between freshman year and now?

BOB: I don't think there is a net change there either. That also might disturb me a little bit. I'm not sure about that. I would like to talk to you about that after this interview.

INTERVIEWER: That will be all right with me. How about the family? Has there been any net change in your relationship with your family between freshman year and senior year?

BOB: No. I certainly have grown to appreciate how fortunate I am in having the family that I do have. They have been really terrific all the way through.

INTERVIEWER: Now, your religious outlook. First of all, you came in with religion—correct me if I am wrong—as one of the major aspects of your life. I have the impression that you are going out with religion still being one of your major concerns. Is that right?

BOB: Yes, that is right.

INTERVIEWER: I would like to have you say something about any changes in the area of religion that have occurred en route; that is, you are not coming out with the same approach or formulation in your mind that you had when you came in, although equal amount of concern?

BOB: That's very true. All that is true. The change that has taken place there is that I had to call into question a lot of—not necessarily my basic beliefs, but the way that my beliefs are practiced and I'm still not set on it. I've come to not place as much importance on the ritual, the formality, of the way religion is practiced in the Episcopal church. Though this is not to say that I do not feel a need for a church as an intermediary thing between myself and my God. I am trying to find a liaison, so to speak, between myself and God, and I am not sure the Episcopal church is it. However, it might be. I'm not sure any church is it.

INTERVIEWER: And that characterizes your present outlook?

BOB: Yes.

INTERVIEWER: Now your political outlook—your political feelings when you came in and that you have now? Has there been essentially any change?

BOB: I'm still a Republican. I am now more acutely aware of the meaning of the Democratic party, and what it has stood for, through history courses. The trouble with me is I haven't had any desire to read the paper every day and to study the developments and trends because I really think in the long run they're all unimportant. I can't feel myself, or I can't bring myself to believe that all these developments that take place day by day and all these editorials and all these columnists and news analysts and all that type of thing are of any lasting value. I like to look at something over a longer period. As a result, I haven't really delved into a lot of the foreign policy issues and domestic policy and all that business of the Republicans as I never did the Democrats. I think in general, basically and resting on the tenets of what the two parties stand for, I came in here a Republican and I leave a Republican.

INTERVIEWER: Do you view your high school experience any differently now from what you thought was worth-while or not worthwhile when you viewed it as a freshman?

BOB: I credit my high school with giving me what we were talking about, a good relationship with guys. I think I came in on a high level. I think, as far as the girls are concerned, I came in on a high level in relationships with them. Intellectually, I did not credit my high school as giving me all that it could have and I'd like to elaborate on that.

INTERVIEWER: Go right ahead.

BOB: They tell you before you come in here that by the end of your sophomore year prep school students and high school students have reached the same level intellectually, that there is no difference between them. That's what they like to think, you know. I feel that a guy with a high school background such as I came from—and it's supposed to be a very good high school in the state of Ohio—can get out of the school only so much, no matter how much you put into it, contrary to what I thought previously. I don't think that a guy coming from a high school has been given a solid enough background intellectually. First of all, he hasn't been given the intellectual drive. I really don't believe that a high school is going to give you an intellectual drive, and as a result, he's not going to be interested intellectually in things until too late, if at all. By too late, I mean up here at least junior year, unless he has it inside himself anyway.

INTERVIEWER: I see.

BOB: A person who does come from a high school is

going to have a reasonably solid background for most colleges. For Princeton, I don't think so. I think that the experience at Princeton is doubly difficult intellectually for a high school student until his senior year and then I think that it probably is the same.

INTERVIEWER: By then he's about caught up on intellectual drive?

BOB: The thing is, you see, the way I feel about it—at least this is true in my case—that I came here freshman year with no intellectual stimulation. I came here just plain to go through four years of school, no particular purpose in mind, just something to do. The foundations for your later college life are laid in your freshman year in these basic over-all general courses that are given and if you don't have any drive in these courses, then you're at a disadvantage all the way through. It doesn't even level off, really, so the guy immediately when he comes here must realize how important freshman year is and sophomore year too—and I don't know that high school gives you that realization.

INTERVIEWER: Now, with what group of groups have you tended to identify yourself? Suppose some outsider were looking down here on the campus and he says, "Oh, I see Bob goes around with this group." What might he say? Not in the way you look at it, but the way an outsider might look at it?

BOB: Well, I think he would tend to say with guys that I do run around with, primarily, I place a high value on the relationship with my roommates. I feel very close to them. However, it's not restricted to them. It's certainly not restricted to Ivy Club. I can name specific individuals who I like to be with—whom I enjoy being with—and I can name them. They would come from . . . from ten clubs.

INTERVIEWER: All right. You have a wide variety of

friends but your closest tend to come from what group
—or don't you see yourself going around with a particular
group, or do you?

BOB: Well, I mean my roommates, I see myself going
around with them.

INTERVIEWER: How would you classify them? That's
really what I am getting at.

BOB: I know but I don't understand that. I mean, I
don't know how you can classify them.

INTERVIEWER: It's not for me to do it. It's just a question
of whether you see it as a classifiable group.

BOB: No, I don't; other people might.

INTERVIEWER: What might *they* say?

BOB: Well, I mean I don't think they would see it as a
group.

INTERVIEWER: What are the characteristics of the group
that you belong to? In other words, is it a group that's
fairly interested in athletics?

BOB: Oh, yes.

INTERVIEWER: That's what I am trying to find out.
What other characteristics can you think of?

BOB: I don't know. If you ask me some questions, I
could answer yes or no.

INTERVIEWER: Well, is it a particularly intellectual
group?

BOB: No.

INTERVIEWER: Is it a group that comes from a lower
economic status primarily or a higher economic status?

BOB: I'd say upper middle class.

INTERVIEWER: Well, compared to the Princeton population, do you think they'd be in the upper half or the
upper quarter?

BOB: Upper half.

INTERVIEWER: Fine. What do you consider to be the
ideal teacher-student relationship?

BOB: Where the student can feel at ease with a person, as he would a friend of the family at home or with a father or one of his friends, say. Not necessarily knowing the personal background of the individual, but interested in the student as an individual, knowing what his activities are—what he's interested in—why he's interested in them—some of the things that have constituted his background.

INTERVIEWER: Other than myself, how many faculty members have you come to know on a personal basis?

BOB: What do you mean by personal basis?

INTERVIEWER: That he knows you, and you are aware that he is interested in you. He knows something about your aspirations and what your strong and weak points are. He may not call you by your first name but you know that he knows your first name.

BOB: Well, there are faculty members who call me by my first name who I don't think have any personal interest in me.

INTERVIEWER: Oh, sure.

BOB: I wouldn't say any. However, I feel that there are certain men I can talk to very freely. I mean, like my thesis supervisor, Professor Fine. He is very interested in me.

INTERVIEWER: Looking at yourself in perspective: relative to the general population—not just the Princeton population, but the general population of people your own age and sex—what has been or are your principal assets or good points, as you see it?

BOB: Oh, an ability to adapt myself to most any situation with people and feel at ease and have the other people know that I am at ease. An ability to get along well with people and talk freely with them. A not unlimited but certainly a wide scope of interests. In other

THE REASONABLE ADVENTURER

words, I am not particularly centralized. I think an over-all athletic ability. I don't know as I can think of any-thing else.

INTERVIEWER: Fine. Now, your liabilities or short-comings? Here again, I don't want you to dig too far—just as it comes readily to your mind.

BOB: An inability to express myself well, written—on paper.

INTERVIEWER: Okay. Who have been the most signifi-cant people in your life?

BOB: My whole life?

INTERVIEWER: By significant I mean that they may have influenced your development in a positive way or in a negative way. But among all the people whom you have been influenced by, whom would you classify among the most significant?

BOB: My parents, definitely. A man named Cliff Drury who is a—head of a camp in Michigan where I went for six years. A fantastic man! Let's see—you. I'd say my roommate, Joe Sugar. I'd also say my grandmother. I guess that's it.

INTERVIEWER: What, if you are aware of any, was the greatest lack in your childhood?

BOB: I don't think I am aware of any. I think I had an ideal childhood. I wouldn't trade it.

INTERVIEWER: Now, briefly, would you discuss your personal ideas on good and evil?

BOB: Briefly?

INTERVIEWER: Well, you can take the next hour and a half if you wish, but I just thought you might at least like a few minutes on it.

BOB: Evil and good. I think it basically rests in the mind. Any action which is considered evil—you're going to find an elaboration on this a little later, when we talk after the interview is over—any action which is considered evil, if it has no malice, absolutely no malice, absolutely pure motives, cannot be considered evil.

INTERVIEWER: In other words, the crucial matter is the motive involved.

BOB: The crucial matter is the motive involved. A good act can be the most evil thing in the world.

As far as evil and good as themselves are concerned, that's awfully difficult to try and state, I mean, it's something that—when you can go into—you can go into religion on that.

INTERVIEWER: What do you think makes life worth living?

BOB: If you have a purpose—life has to have a purpose, it has to have an end—maybe this is twentieth-century United States utilitarianism, I don't know, but if life for you has a purpose, you're here for a purpose and if you do not devote your life to yourself but you are living it for some thing or someone else, be it a person or be it a God, or be it a principle, if you have the purpose in mind and if you—the purpose is not yourself, then your life, I think, no matter how it is lived, is going to be worth living.

INTERVIEWER: Even though it may not have been a difficult decision, looking back on your life, what do you think is your most important decision?

BOB: I don't know as I can pick one out—one outstanding decision that I've made.

INTERVIEWER: Even though it may not have been an important decision, what do you remember as your most *difficult* decision?

BOB: Giving up football freshman year.

INTERVIEWER: Oh, yes. I remember that. Incidentally, do you feel you made the right decision?

BOB: In the long run, yes.

INTERVIEWER: Were you sorry you had to make that decision?

BOB: Yes.

INTERVIEWER: What type of work do you think you'll be engaged in? What sort of role do you think you will take?

BOB: I think I will be engaged in just business. I am going to be one of those business men, I think.

INTERVIEWER: What will be your hobbies and outside interests?

BOB: Athletics.

INTERVIEWER: Anything else you might do in your spare time?

BOB: I'll probably work on community projects and interests, things like that. I am going to be a golf man. I am going to take my kids to baseball games all the time, and I am going to be in a bowling league and I am going to be active in church. I am going to be a typical American.

Michael—Late Senior Year

INTERVIEWER: How do you feel about your thesis, Michael, now that it's done?

MICHAEL: I wish that I had picked a subject much earlier, picked a subject that I really liked, and then really settled down to work on it. I think it can be a very rewarding experience if you end up doing something that really means something to you. As it turned out, the subject I chose was not the most interesting of subjects. I didn't get started on it till the end. In fact, I wrote the thing from April 2 to May 2 and I redid all my research practically. I wasted a great opportunity. But I am all in favor of having to write them.

INTERVIEWER: Why do you think that the thesis is a good idea?

MICHAEL: I think you really feel as though you have done something when you finish them. I think it gives you a head start on people, those who have never written a thesis. Pretty big production when you think about it. Mine was 40,000 words. You feel as though you have created something.

INTERVIEWER: Can you tell me what particular aspect of writing a thesis gave you special satisfaction?

MICHAEL: Well, the hardest thing for me is to write. The best feeling is after I have written, because I have a hell of a job writing, and then when I finish, it's usually fairly—pretty good. Like I just finished a paper yesterday, Friday, on a SPIA (School of Public and International Affairs) conference that we just finished having. I had a *hell* of a time getting that paper written! I mean it was really a task, real labor. Don Bear wrote his in a morning and an afternoon; just sat down and dashed it off. I slaved over it for about five or six days! But it's a great feeling when you are finished, and the fact you got this idea across.

INTERVIEWER: It sounds very good. You really have to work at it. Is it working at it in the sense of getting up steam? Or really working at it to complete it?

MICHAEL: Well, first of all, I have trouble getting started. I can never start writing till I absolutely have to, usually.

And then I have to get in the mood to write. I just can't sit down any time and start writing. And then when I do sit down, I usually have trouble thinking. I know what I want to say but I don't know how to say it. Or something like this: I have all my ideas, and I can't get them down fast enough, and I forget them before I can write them down. That's why I am going to learn to type. This happens to me: I think of two sentences I am going to say, my next two thoughts, and by the time I finish writing one sentence, I forget what my next thought was. This happens to me all the time.

INTERVIEWER: Don't you ever compose things when you are walking down the street?

MICHAEL: No, in fact I sit down with a piece of paper, and before I write the first word, I don't know what the second one is going to be, either. Then I just start writing, and it just starts coming. It just follows right along. That's when I can really write.

INTERVIEWER: What was the relationship between you and your supervisor?

MICHAEL: No relationship at all. I mean, I had trouble getting a topic, and I didn't go to see him once, from the time I got my topic till I went to ask for an extension of time. I hadn't been in to see him once. I had no supervision at all. I didn't go to ask for it, and he never wrote me or anything. It was strictly done completely on my own. It was independent in every sense of the word.

INTERVIEWER: Now, looking at your four years here in perspective, what experiences have you had that you think have contributed most to your development—real development? That is, every time you went through a period like this, you felt that you had really changed for the better, either in your outlook or your . . .

MICHAEL: Well, the fellowship interviews, definitely.

INTERVIEWER: Yes.

MICHAEL: I mean, of all the things I did this year, I think this probably more than anything else. Not getting it or anything, but just going—well, yes, getting it because it made the whole thing successful. It showed that it had worked. Writing a senior thesis, I think, helped me to grow; taking final exams, or taking any exams. Final exams were great, for a while. I love to take an exam if I have enough time to study for it.

INTERVIEWER: Yes.

MICHAEL: I get right down there 'fore the exam and— I can sort of remember last year, I went into the exam and you know you know the stuff, cold. You've been through the course. You know you've gotten on the inside and you're looking out.

INTERVIEWER: Yes.

MICHAEL: And boy, you're tying things together that you know that probably very few other guys are doing. You are really into the heart of the course. Then you go in, and take an exam and they'll ask you a question. See, my trouble is, I can't outline. This goes back again to the way I write, as I told you before. I don't compose ahead of time. I just start writing and then it starts to come. I think of the ideas as I go, sort of. But to take a final exam, all of a sudden you have an insight, and then you write this down. I really think this has been developed.

I think I have a greater awareness of the value and the importance of the humanities, and I'm getting this a little more and more. I have had some courses in the last couple of years which have gotten this across to me. I think I am sort of getting a little bit of a bent in this direction, but it's mainly still in the social sciences.

I think this place has been great for me, intellectually. I mean really good. I don't think I would have gotten it elsewhere. In a non-Ivy League or a non-Big Three school.

INTERVIEWER: How about your relationship with other students?

MICHAEL: Is this from freshman year to now?

INTERVIEWER: Yes. How close were you with guys your own age then, compared to your closeness now?

MICHAEL: Well, I think that my relationship with my close friends is pretty much the same, although those who may be my close friends are changing. I think the relationship with the peripheral group is better. I'm more aware that a person on the peripheral group may move into the close group, I think, than I was as a freshman. I'm not sure about this. And I am more inclined to include more people in the peripheral group, of these guys here in Princeton.

INTERVIEWER: There has been a greater mobility.

MICHAEL: Yes, very definitely.

INTERVIEWER: That is, of getting to know a guy better. The opportunity to get to know a guy better is so much easier now than it was freshman year.

MICHAEL: My relationships with girls are not good I don't think. I haven't had enough experience, actually. Relationships with the family are much better. Well, yes, I think they are better. I really feel bad now that I didn't do a lot of things before; I really treated my family lousy when you come down to it. As far as including them in my education in Princeton as an insider rather than an outsider. And they really don't understand what a lot of things mean, which they could have understood. But the trouble was that I never knew, back then, what would come eventually. And so when the things began to come, it was too late to bring them in.

INTERVIEWER: Now your religious outlook. Do you think you were as interested in it freshman year, or more now?

MICHAEL: I think I am more interested in it now than I was then. But only because it has been raised as a problem to me in the course of my going through here. I had a good religious course this past term with this guy Chadwick.

INTERVIEWER: Yes.

MICHAEL: He really did a good job.

INTERVIEWER: So that intellectually you understand religion better.

MICHAEL: I pray when I get in trouble, always. I tend to feel somewhat jerky about it but I don't really feel guilty about it, in a way. I feel two ways about it. I feel that I prayed and God came through, and then I feel that I deserved it all the time anyhow.

INTERVIEWER: Yes. You aren't so sure just . . .

MICHAEL: Yes. Then I feel I could have done it anyhow, but just to be sure I'd better pray to God.

INTERVIEWER: Yes, well, it's a question of pulling out all the stops.

MICHAEL: Yes. And yet, when I talk like this I feel that maybe this will get God mad, see.

INTERVIEWER: You had better be careful.

MICHAEL: Well, it's just as bad to think it, because God would know if·I were thinking it. But then I figure, the fact that I know that this is not particularly good will then excuse me as far as God is concerned.

INTERVIEWER: So . . .

MICHAEL: I'm not very religious.

INTERVIEWER: How about your political outlook?

MICHAEL: It *has* changed.

INTERVIEWER: Okay. Do you want to say what the change has been?

MICHAEL: Well, I was always for Roosevelt but now I know why I was for Roosevelt. I'm a free enterprise man. I think by conviction as well as practically.

INTERVIEWER: What do you think is the ideal teacher-student relationship? Whether you've experienced it or not, what do you think is the ideal?

MICHAEL: Well, I think you sorta ought to idolize a teacher, and idolize what he teaches too, in a sense. The teacher should be warned well, and should know that the way he treats you is important to you and that when he just sort of steps all over you, it really hurts.

My notion of what an ideal teacher-student relationship is—I don't know. It is changing. I think it is changing away from the idol idea to one of more of interaction.

INTERVIEWER: Of more of a collateral relationship.

MICHAEL: Of an interchange with the realization that this guy has more knowledge than you, but that you have something to give this guy too.

I think it's changing—sorta the teacher knows more but that you also have something to offer to the teacher too, maybe, rather than this—coming down from on high like.

INTERVIEWER: Rather than sitting . . .

MICHAEL: In that sense, I think, what I said at first is not right—that I don't consider that the ideal student-teacher relationship.

INTERVIEWER: Now your life in perspective. Relative to the general population what are or have been your principal assets or good points? This is, of course, putting all modesty aside.

MICHAEL: My ability to talk to people.

INTERVIEWER: Ability to get other people to warm up to you?

MICHAEL: Yes. But, you see, I think I do this schemingly because I can feel when I go into a group that I could say—now if I said this or if I go along this way, this will be the right way, but if I do that, that will be the wrong way.

INTERVIEWER: Well, any other assets?

MICHAEL: Memory, I think I remember things pretty well.

INTERVIEWER: Now do you want to go into liabilities? Shortcomings if any?

MICHAEL: Well, I feel shortcomings in social talents. Would this fit in here? Is this where it should go?

INTERVIEWER: Yes.

MICHAEL: I sort of feel a social inability.

INTERVIEWER: Okay. Would you discuss briefly your

personal ideas on good and evil. Don't take too long on it.

MICHAEL: Well, I think people are good, basically. Is this the idea, sort of?

INTERVIEWER: Yes.

MICHAEL: I don't really think that a person is bad because he didn't get the good breaks, I mean the good opportunities. Although, again I think I am becoming a little less of an absolutist on this thing and am moving away toward—perhaps if some people are, falling down, you know. A lot of this is coming in in my education I think.

INTERVIEWER: Well, do you have anything in mind of what you consider good, and what sort of things you would consider evil?

MICHAEL: Yes, well I think Christ was a good person because he is the kind of person who can criticize someone but when he criticizes them he has a respect for them too at the same time that he criticizes them. And he realizes that these people deserve an opportunity just as much as he does. They are like fingers on your hand—they're all united underneath with just little popping outs of the one will underneath.

I sort of feel that—I love that poem, the one about the bell tolls for thee when it tolls for everyone else idea.

The good person believes that everybody has a certain dignity and he believes that each person ought to have a chance to really express himself and this is why I am a small D democrat because I think that democracy gives people a respect for the person and that it also gives a person the greatest opportunity to express himself. I don't think one person should be able to tell another person what to do. I think that the majority should be able to tell the minority what to do so long as the minority has a chance to become a majority and later can tell others what to do. I don't think that anyone should always serve someone else, although they may at any one particular time. It's sort of because they agree to a process by which they pick someone to do the deciding for them. I don't know, you can't let people suffer. I don't think suffering is good for people. The way some people try to tell you, you know, this is good, it builds character type of thing. I think a challenge is but not suffering like. This is something I really think I believe deeply. I think I believe in it emotionally primarily, rather than intellectually.

INTERVIEWER: And I think it is something you came to Princeton with.

MICHAEL: I think I got it from my father.

INTERVIEWER: What do you think makes life worth living?

MICHAEL: I think the chance to do something for someone else, instead of sort of doing it for yourself. My one-word answer would be *people*. Well, it would deal with people. I have to have a job where I will go out and talk to people and try to show them what I think is right and why this is the best thing you should do. Try to help them, show them that if we do this it would be better for everyone concerned.

INTERVIEWER: Now, if and when you are a parent, what would you most like to teach your children?

MICHAEL: I'd like—one of the things, I don't know whether I can say most, maybe I ought to say some of the things and then I can pick out the one most, I would like to teach my children to be tough but not to be a bastard about it. I would want my kid to be the sort of kid that when a kid is getting picked on in a playground by the bully, my kid would come along and beat the hell out of the bully, see, but that my kid would never pick on the kids that were less strong than he, but that whenever these kids who were less strong than he got into trouble he came along and helped them. But at the same time that he beat up the bully, he shouldn't hate the bully completely. He should only hate the bully for what he had done, but realizing that maybe the bully wasn't such a bad guy either. That would be one of the things, I think.

INTERVIEWER: Toughness with charity.

MICHAEL: Yes, sort of.

INTERVIEWER: Or love.

MICHAEL: Well, I think this is sort of the idea. I would like to teach him this idea of . . . that each person does have a certain worth and a certain dignity. That perhaps we are all in it together and the thing that we should do is try and develop a sort of situation in which we can all progress together too. I don't want my kid to be stingy, I want him to be willing to share, you know, with other kids. I would sort of like him to be for the underdog all the time. This is, I think, one of the reasons I like Roosevelt so much because I always felt he was for the underdogs.

Don—Late Senior Year

INTERVIEWER: How do you feel about your thesis now that it's done?

DON: Well, I feel pretty good about it. I don't know yet what I got on it but I imagine either a 1 (A) or 1— (A—), probably a 1. I started out in the fall knowing I wanted to do an experimental thesis and that I wanted to do it for one of two men: either Fankhauser or Pittendrigh in Bio, and I decided on Fankhauser. I went to see him and we shot the bull for about an hour, I guess, about what I wanted to do in medicine and so forth and so on; what I'd done in the past. Then he more or less gave me a topic, and I decided to take it; and essentially it was a matter of procrastination from there until spring vacation.

INTERVIEWER: Do you want to say what your topic is?

DON: Yes, it is an introductory study of the Mauthner apparatus. As I just said, it was a matter of procrastination from then till spring. All fall I was pretty much involved with the Refreshment Agency (a stadium concession), and all I did was to catch my animals and try to set up a couple of experiments, one of which never worked out. So I had to devise a secondary means of doing approximately the same thing, altering the swimming, or the amount of swimming, the animals would undergo. This was to see what effects that might have on the growth of these specialized nerve cells. The other large experiment was to see how the cell grew in relation to body growth. I didn't do very much. I learned histological technique and so forth during the fall, but largely I just put things off. I did a little library research but not an awful lot; and then when I came back from Christmas vacation, it was pretty much a straight grind for midyear exams. Between exams I did a little bit, but not much between exams and the new term. Then when the second term started, it was Bicker (eating club elections) for three weeks, and also a few other problems concerning the administration and so forth. Then it was studying for midterms and so forth.

Finally this term I've been working pretty damn steadily on it; but the biggest bulk of the work came with spring vacation. I figured I could knock it off over spring vacation, which was a fantastic dream. I worked like hell and I stayed here all the time. I'd go for three days with a meal a day and about four or five hours' sleep. I was making all my slides then; I guess I have slides for about a hundred and twenty animals. About the time spring vacation was over, I started to study them, and I found some new methods for studying and making quantitative comparisons of cell size and so forth. It all took a hell of a lot of time, and the damn thing just turned out to be a monster. I decided to take photographs to make some of the things more apparent, and ran up to eighty-five photomicrographs. Then I started trying to write my introduction which essentially consisted of a review of the past literature. I was semi-interested in it, I suppose, but then when things started getting complicated, it started getting interesting, and I had to work the damn thing out. I wasn't going to let it go through sort of halfbaked and so I really bore down on the thing. Now, I'm pretty damn proud of it. It was a lot of work, and I really feel it paid off. I think I got quite a bit out of it: I know a lot better how to set up an experiment. The real thing is posing a problem and cutting out all the variables which I didn't do.

INTERVIEWER: Good. Now what do you think of your four years here in terms of deep satisfaction, in terms of personal growth and development?

DON: I think there have been several things here. One of them, I think, is just sort of the feeling of having grown. It's like I used to say in freshman year, I think, that life is pretty rich; there's nothing more pleasant than feeling you've had a deep experience. When you listen to someone like Governor Stevenson you just sort of have chills up your spine, and really feel close to the experience he is relating, as if you've been a part of it. A lot of satisfaction came in the social area, the Bicker, the feeling of being able to maintain a certain amount of democratic spirit throughout the Bicker, really getting fairly close to a number of guys and working with them, and sharing a lot of mutual respect for others' opinions.

I think, particularly in the last year, there has been a lot of satisfaction in the intellectual realm which had never really been allowed a chance to flourish, in a way.

INTERVIEWER: Now, your intellectual life. Consider what your involvements and interests were in your freshman year in contrast to the way it appears now and whether it's changed.

DON: In freshman year I regarded my previous approach to schoolwork as a failure to take opportunities that presented themselves both in and out of school. Then in freshman year I sort of set myself out on an idealistic plane of—the hell with grades, the important thing is to learn, whether I learn it from a book or whether I learn it from experience. An example of this is that one day I just said, "The hell with classes," and went out with a group to see the United Nations. I think my new exuberance for extrascholastic experiences tapered when I started having emotional problems about a girl that I had to handle during freshman year.

By the end of freshman year I had pretty well decided I wanted to go into medicine, and from then on my efforts have been pretty much confined to that, although some of the courses that I got the greatest enjoyment out of weren't directly related to medicine, for example, cultural anthropology. I think the big change, intellectually, has been more natural—almost excitement in certain areas of study and a desire to continue to broaden.

In freshman year I would probably have liked to pursue art or philosophy, but it would have been more for the sake of being broadened than for their own sake.

INTERVIEWER: Yes. Now it's more for their own sake.

DON: Yes. Now I can see how I could really enjoy becoming wrapped up in any one of them.

INTERVIEWER: Can you make a similar comparison or contrast between freshman and senior years in the area of relationships with your peers, those of your own age and sex?

DON: I think there is a lot more feedback on my relationships. I have a more accurate appraisal of who's a friend and what sort of friend and how close. I think now in the last half year, I've been narrowing more and more whereas earlier I was trying to broaden more and more in a number of friends. I think now there's more of an emphasis on the fundamental beliefs of the two—or the enjoyment the two get out of looking at each other's completely different ideas. The basis for a friendship is different in a way. It isn't so much based on outward achievement in athletic success or success in any particular area, but more of the type of person, the way he views other people and the way he approaches his problems. I mean, it's become really important that a person's ideas have been found out by his own thought and not by someone else's. It is important that a person be openminded and not dogmatic for any sort of a deep friendship.

INTERVIEWER: All right. Now are you ready to go on about women?

DON: This is a hell of a time in view of recent circumstances to try and get a really rational point of view on this topic. The growth in the four years has been fantastic. Freshman year, what a beautiful love I had! It was one of the blindest, most all-consuming . . . but really blind. And then when that went down the drain I really went into the depths.

INTERVIEWER: When did it go down the drain?

DON: Right after Christmas, freshman year. But of course I couldn't accept it as going down then. It wasn't until about eight months later that I accepted the fact that it was finished.

INTERVIEWER: You are not married now, but what would you say was important in a marriage relationship?

DON: Well, I guess the first factor is that which offers the primary sort of—not enjoyment, that isn't enough of a word—values in life, which give you the feeling of rich experiences. Another factor is having essentially the same ideas about children and working together, the real enjoyment of doing things together, and similarity in a healthy attitude toward sex.

INTERVIEWER: Do you want to go into any change in your relationship with your family between freshman year and now?

DON: There's been a lot more interaction between my father and me. We've talked about a lot more things, and there's been a real change since I was a little kid. I just couldn't argue with him then. I mean, if he said something and I disagreed with him, I was off to my room and sulking or crying and just thinking he was completely unfair and so forth. Then there was a period of, instead of reaction, rather hiding things;. in other words, not bringing up problems, but knowing that I was handling them right. Now it's more the period of . . . there's a lot more assertion on my part of what I'm going to do.

INTERVIEWER: Have your relationships with your mother been pretty consistent?

DON: Yes, I think so. I think they've been pretty constant ever since I was small. Much warmth and companionship.

INTERVIEWER: What have been the changes in your religious outlook between freshman year and now?

DON: Well, as far as my own religion goes, it's essentially the same: a lack thereof. I think there has been a growth in understanding of religion as a whole and of other people's personal religions. I don't think there's been any real change in my own mind. I think intellectually I've been an agnostic and emotionally an atheist; and I think that is pretty similar to my views in freshman year. Although I may not have verbalized it that way, this is what I feel now very strongly.

INTERVIEWER: In other words, regardless of your point of view, religion has been a significant area of your life?

DON: Yes, definitely. I have a lot of pride in my own

feelings, my intellectualizations and my stand. I think I see more humor in it now than I ever did before, too. I am amused by the Catholic who is pretty rational in most aspects, but the moment something touches on any of the dogma, he becomes completely irrational and can't argue clearly. About a year ago I read an article on agnosticism by Bertrand Russell, and although I've only looked at it once since, it's almost become a bible for me. My religious position is sort of an outgrowth of just my way of life. I prefer to take a more objective stand rather than one where you can't set up any means to verification. I find for myself, at least, that the agnostic position lends more thought to why we act the way we do. Consequently, you have a firmer basis for action than when you do it because of Someone Else rather than because this is what you believe.

INTERVIEWER: Yes. Has there been any change in your political outlook between freshman and senior years?

DON: Well, the main change has been one of degree of interest, in which it's broadened a great deal; formerly, more just an emotional interest and whether we were able to defeat the Nazis, or fight communism, or get the best man for president. Whereas now, it's much more of a real concern for the world, in a way; seeing and understanding more the way the local, national, and international politics all fit in together and depend upon each other, and the matter now of taking pretty strong positions on certain things such as McCarthy and the differences between Democratic and Republican platforms, the differences in the outlook of the men that represent them. Then at times, I have sort of a schizophrenic intellectualization of the whole damn thing: the international strife and so forth in which it becomes impossible to see how in the hell it can all be so damn messed up. With a basic belief in the dignity of each individual and a real sort of belief in the worth of each person, I am just wondering how in the hell, if everybody essentially has the same attitudes, they can be so prostituted as to line people up on different sides of the fence. It's the same old useless argument—if nobody wants war, why does it ever happen?

INTERVIEWER: Now, has there been any change in your ideal of friendship—what you thought should occur in a friendship; your criterion of a friendship between freshman year and now?

DON: I'm not sure because I can't remember too well what my criteria were then, but I still, I suppose, put a lot of emphasis on the loyalty aspects but I also put a lot of emphasis on, probably even more so than I did before, the amount of communication of basic feelings, the amount of ability to understand the other person, even when his actions seem the most removed from what you would expect them to be, or what you'd hope them to be.

INTERVIEWER: What do you consider to be the ideal teacher-student relationship?

DON: One of equality, to begin with, and a mutual respect and appreciation of the other person's ideas even if they're completely different. One in which a person feels he can really let himself loose, and without regard to whatever implications it might have; ability on the part of the student to tell the teacher who might be considered to be an authority that he's full of crap; and at the same time, an ability on the part of the teacher to understand that. Dr. Chiquoine in biology seems to me to be the perfect university teacher. He really knows his field. He's interested in students' learning; not in just presenting things that he knows. He's really interested in the students. He's young and he understands them, and you feel you are his equal. He doesn't ever make you feel subservient.

INTERVIEWER: Now your life in perspective: relative to

the general population of people in the country of your own sex, what are or have been your principal assets or good points?

DON: Well, first is intelligence. I think I've been pretty fortunate there, I'd guess an I.Q. of about 120. And second would be opportunity, stemming from two intelligent and wise parents and an educational opportunity from a good financial basis, upper middle class. I think the whole emotional development has been a pretty fortunate one; the whole family situation having been good, having had good opportunities for friendship and so forth.

INTERVIEWER: Now, liabilities or shortcomings?

DON: Well, I'd say probably my liabilities were predominantly in the personality field in which with some insecurity compensated for by a certain amount of rigidity and, at certain periods during my life, a sort of hazy understanding of the environment. Usually this goes on for a couple of years in which I feel my situation out. Then, finally, the pattern would come that I want to fit, and then I would shape the environment sort of, really come to understand it in terms of life objectives and in terms of the present situation. Prep school was one place where I saw this happen, and here was another. I find that in dealing with a new situation my attempts are average or below average, but once I've gone through it a couple of times, I find that they're above average. It's a matter of practice and then perfecting. So, I'd say the liability there would be an inefficiency in exploratory activity, but once time has been allowed for sufficient exploration without my having particularly caused it, why then once I understand the thing, I can handle it.

INTERVIEWER: Very good.

DON: And also a necessity for building up a security basis before I can flow.

INTERVIEWER: Yes.

DON: Like, well just take academics here, once I became involved in a lot of things and had a pretty good emotional base, then I could flow much better. My grades came easily without my even trying; whereas, before I'd try like hell, and it would come hard.

INTERVIEWER: Sure.

DON: Whereas, previously I could do every assignment for every course and know the things backwards and forwards and louse it up; now I can do twice the assignments and in half the time and do better.

INTERVIEWER: Now your inner-self is participating.

DON: Yes.

INTERVIEWER: What would you say was the greatest lack in your childhood, if any?

DON: Oh, a good question! Somehow, somewhere along the way I lacked a push that would make me really understand my environment. I look back now—I've said this before, maybe in slightly different words—there's sort of a period of years there that are all sort of hazy. I mean, as I put myself back at age seven or whatever, when I look out, I see sort of a haze around me instead of what I now see is there. Actually, I don't know what was lacking to make this the situation, but I see that I was just sort of groping in a way. It's hard to express it because I have it more as a feeling than an intellectualization.

INTERVIEWER: Yes. What about this haze? You say there's a haze over what period?

DON: Well, it isn't a haze over a period. It's a period of haze that, well, I can sort of make an analogy with poor eyesight, sort of . . .

INTERVIEWER: Oh, a period of hazy *perception*.

DON: Yes, and not understanding.

INTERVIEWER: In other words, it isn't the fact that this whole period is hazy?

DON: Oh no, far from it.

INTERVIEWER: It's a period of your life when your perceptions were hazy?

DON: Yes, that's it!

Yes, more the latter. I don't see it as a focusing of perception in which I excluded a lot. It was more that the things came in, but I didn't react. I can see the environmental stimuli that were there and I can see now how I wish to hell I'd reacted with more participation in certain things.

INTERVIEWER: You can't understand why you reacted the way you did?

DON: Yes. But I don't see what it was that was lacking to make this the case. I don't know how to clarify it either.

INTERVIEWER: How long was this period?

DON: I'm not really sure. I would say the major portion of it probably started around the first grade and probably ran, where the fog was the thickest, to about the sixth grade. Then it began to clear, sort of, and I could see through the haze for a while, through maybe the ninth grade. Then it sort of set in again with my change in schools. Then it cleared up in about a year and from then on it's become less and less of a haze. I'd say it is now probably starting last spring, sort of clear vision instead of any haze at all.

INTERVIEWER: All right. Would you discuss now briefly your personal ideas on good and evil?

DON: I believe pretty much in the unwritten law of *Mens rea.*

INTERVIEWER: Of what?

DON: *Mens rea;* the concept that intent is what is important rather than action. In other words, in some cultures a person is equally guilty if he accidentally kills his wife or if he purposely does so. I think the motive is in my mind the real determinant plus an understanding of the psychological background of the individual. In other words, I don't see any absolute values at all here, as far as being able to judge acts as being worthy or unworthy. I have a conflict in the realm of means and ends relationships. I mean, I certainly don't hold as absolutely as some religions would purport to, that something is good only if its means are thoroughly good. I feel the ends are very important here too. I think that good and evil depend very much upon the way a person feels about what he is doing, as well as whatever unconscious motivations may be present. In other words, if unconsciously he is trying to do what consciously he would consider evil, it still may not be evil, as long as he doesn't feel it is so. I think that's essentially it. Each act or thought or deed has to be judged in context.

In some cases I think the means are more important, and in others I feel the end is more important. I can't break down the two as to which cases I feel one is more important than the other. It's the same thing with the act and the motivations. I suppose they are both important.

In other words, an act could have severely damaging consequences for everybody but the individual and, therefore, be bad but at the same time, the person could be good because this was the opposite of his intent.

INTERVIEWER: What do you think makes life worth living?

DON: Two things: one, the belief in tomorrow, and the other, enjoyment in the act of living today.

INTERVIEWER: Well, when you've finished your education and you've settled down in your work, where and in what kind of place will you probably live? What part of the country?

DON: I will probably live in Los Angeles—or southern California, I suppose, and whether I live in the country or city or small town or what, will depend upon, in part, what specialty I undertake and so forth. If I go into psychiatry, I'll remain, or probably will remain in close contact with a big city so that I can practice in the city. I'd like to live in a locality such that I was outside a small town, in the country and have land and a house, not just a house on a small lot. At the same time, I want to be part of a small community in which there will be sufficient and plentiful children as playmates for my children. And at the same time, this small community should both be isolated and connected with a large city, isolated to the extent that the interpersonal relationships remain within the community, but connected with a large city to the extent that for supplies and things like theatre and so forth, one wouldn't have a strain of getting to it. This is sort of an idealization of what I'd like. Whether or not I'll find it, I don't know, but I think I'd like to live in the sort of climate which does not have great seasonal differences. I don't particularly enjoy the slush and the snow and so forth. I'd rather live in a very temperate climate.

INTERVIEWER: What kind of household atmosphere would you like to have?

DON: Permissive. And one in which there's a real closeness in the family and yet an atmosphere in which anyone could disagree or whatever he wished and not feel that he's going to hurt someone else for it!

INTERVIEWER: What type of work will you be engaged in and what sort of role will you take?

DON: I'll be engaged in medicine, and I hope to take a competent role.

INTERVIEWER: Now, what are the fields of medicine that are right now under consideration?

DON: Primarily psychiatry and pediatrics, with psychiatry pretty far out in front. What I'd really like to do, although it's impossible, is to be a general practitioner with side specialties in psychiatry, pediatrics, and surgery.

INTERVIEWER: Right.

DON: In other words, in a lot of ways, I'd really like to be a general practitioner, but there are certain areas in which I wouldn't get as much pleasure as in other areas, so I'd like to concentrate more on those; or maybe because of this I ought to go into internal medicine but I want to give more of an emphasis to psychiatry than that would allow.

INTERVIEWER: What aspect of the work do you think will give you the most satisfaction?

DON: Helping people. I really want the feeling of being needed in a sense and being competent to help the other individual when he's in pain. I've gotten a great deal of pleasure previously in helping animals in a tough spot, and I'd feel sort of the same thing towards humans, only more so, because of a greater chance for identification and a perception of growth in the individual and overcoming whatever problems he might have, and the perception of whatever I may have done to him.

INTERVIEWER: What would be your hobbies and outside interests?

DON: Well, definitely one of them is going to deal with natural history and particularly with herpetology. When I gave up the idea of going into herpetology I realized that it'd never be too far away because I'd always keep pets. I imagine, well, if I can't afford it, probably what I'd do would be to have one pet at one time and another at another, probably quite different sorts of animals. If I could afford it, I'd like to have a lot of different kinds all at once. I think other interests will be sort of sidelined through my profession. In other words, I want to keep up in medicine. I like the idea of going back to school maybe every five years or something, to get sort of a refresher course on the latest things that have come out. I don't know whether I'll be the kind of doctor that will do that or not. I hope so. But whether I do or not, I imagine I'll keep myself fairly well informed with journals and so forth and I know damn good and well that every once in a while something's going to interest me, and I know I'll try and pursue it a little bit in a sort of research fashion. I think I'll probably always have an interest in keeping my home in good shape, in carpentry and repair work, and building things. Perhaps sometime I'll return to painting, I don't know. I did that as a kid and I used to get a lot of enjoyment out of it. Then I just didn't like it for a long time. Then a couple of months ago I started drawing while I was in a boring seminar or something and I really got a kick out of it. It was better than I expected it to be. I think, maybe sometimes when I have a hell of a problem on my mind, I can probably sit down and draw something and get it out a little bit.

INTERVIEWER: I'm glad that you brought that up.

DON: Well, it's funny, I never really understood why I quit painting. I never did a lot of it, but I sort of felt that I'd quit it even though I'd hardly started. Then when I was talking with Dr. Whipple about med school, I guess when I was a sophomore, why he asked me what some of my hobbies and interests had been, and he really gave me hell for giving up painting. He said this sort of thing is really a tremendous vent for a doctor. I didn't think very much of it at the time, but since then I've just sort of become interested in the idea. And I think, I hope, to maintain a pretty strong interest in community and public affairs.

INTERVIEWER: How about reading? Areas of reading?

DON: Well, there are probably a million books I'd like to read. What happens with me is if I sit down and start reading a book and get into it, I really love it and can't put it down. But I occupy myself with a lot of other things, and a book that I know is good can be lying there and I won't pay any attention to it until I've started it and then

I really enjoy it. Often this comes in spurts too. When I have a lack for something to do, or maybe am in a depressed mood or something, I enjoy doing a lot of reading, and sometimes I'll read three and four books in a row. I imagine I'll read quite a bit. I certainly hope so.

INTERVIEWER: Yesterday was graduation, Don. Do you have your final thoughts on Princeton?

DON: I really love Princeton—God, yes. It didn't hit me until yesterday afternoon about five o'clock, I guess right after I had said goodbye to Tyke, that the goddamn place really got to me. I broke down. Barbara and I were walking along, we were going over to Jeff's room, and Christ! I just couldn't talk for about five minutes . . . so I really feel its closeness.

INTERVIEWER: Thanks very much, Don.

DON: I've enjoyed it very much. It's been a great association.

Appendix B

Notes on Methodology

The Selection of the Sample

Thirty-one members of the Advisee Project comprise a stratified sample of the 625 liberal arts candidates of the Class of 1954. The sample was drawn in July 1950 in the following manner:

I. Each of the 625 students was classified in one of three categories on the following four variables:

A. *Public vs private school preparation*

1. Student spent at least junior and senior year in a public high school

2. Student had experience in both a public and a private school in junior and senior year

3. Student spent at least junior and senior year in a private independent school

B *Financial support*

1. Student receiving scholarship aid and committed to remunerative work on campus

2. Student receiving scholarship aid but not committed to remunerative work on campus

3. Student receiving no aid or assigned work by the University

C. *Family association with Princeton*

1. Student a son of a Princeton alumnus

2. Student not a Princeton son but brother or nephew of a Princeton student or alumnus

3. Student has no close relatives among student or alumni body

D. *Leadership and extracurricular participation in secondary school*

1. Leader in extracurricular activities (i.e., class officer, editor of student paper or yearbook, or major sport captain)

2. Active in extracurricular activities but not a leader (as defined in No. 1 above)

3. Inactive in extracurricular activities

II. All students in category No. 2 of each of the four variables were eliminated from further consideration.

III. The remaining students, i.e., those in categories 1 and 3 for each variable, were assigned to statistical cells of identical classification in terms of category and variable. For example, all private school, no aid or work, Princeton son and extracurricular leaders were assigned to the same cell. Since the number of students in each cell varied, a table of random numbers was used to select the sample for the experimental and control groups. The sample was selected in a stratified manner to closely approximate the class as a whole. An exception was made, however, in regard to variable C, family association with Princeton. Additional weight was given to this variable (nearly one-third of the sample) to permit more adequate comparison with non-Princeton sons should this be needed. Only one-fifth of the liberal arts students in the class were Princeton sons.

This sampling procedure yielded thirty-one cases in each group, the experimental and the control. For West Coast representation, three students were added to the experimental group. Also added to this group were two students living near Princeton, New Jersey, in the summer of 1950 who were studied first for purposes of testing the adequacy of the proposed prematriculation standardized interview. The final outcome, therefore, was thirty-six cases.

Determining a Student's Position in Model

A student's place in the model was determined by the intersection of his position on the two dimensions of the model, the developmental and the temperamental. A person's position on the developmental scale (distance from point A) involved the use of three psychological rating scales:

Scale I—Satisfaction from academic work
Scale II—Satisfaction from friendship with peers
Scale III—Self-understanding and acceptance

Each scale is a five-point scale. If, for example, a student is rated a '2' on all three scales his total score on the developmental dimension would be six points. Total scores can range, therefore, from three to fifteen points. For illustrative purposes it may interest the reader to see the developmental dimensions scores of Bob, Michael, and Don broken down by scale ratings for the four years in college. The rating period for freshman year was in December while the remaining three periods were in May. Table 4 portrays this:

TABLE 4.

Developmental Scale Ratings of Three Students

| | Bob | | | | Michael | | | | Don | | | |
	I	II	III	Total	I	II	III	Total	I	II	III	Total
Freshman	1.5	3.0	2.5	7.0	2.0	2.5	2.0	6.5	2.0	2.0	2.0	6.0
Sophomore	2.5	4.0	3.0	9.5	3.0	3.0	3.0	9.0	2.5	2.5	2.0	7.0
Junior	2.5	3.0	3.0	8.5	3.5	4.0	3.0	10.5	3.0	4.0	3.0	10.0
Senior	3.0	3.5	3.5	10.0	4.0	4.0	4.0	12.0	3.5	4.0	3.5	11.0

Looking at the project as a whole, Table 5 summarizes the four-year growth progression of the twenty-eight graduating students on the three developmental scales. It

THE REASONABLE ADVENTURER

may be noted that the greatest gain was in the area of intrinsic interest in academic work. Growth in depth of interpersonal relations and degree of self-acceptance was less on the average but still substantial.

TABLE 5.

Mean Developmental Progression of Graduating Group (N = 28)

RATING PERIOD	I	II	III	TOTAL
Freshman (Dec. 1950)	2.14	2.50	2.36	7.00
Sophomore (May 1952)	3.01	3.14	2.80	8.95
Junior (May 1953)	3.09	3.32	3.07	9.48
Senior (May 1954)	3.50	3.59	3.32	10.41
Net Change	1.36	1.09	0.96	3.41

Scale I—*Satisfaction from academic work*

1. No evidence of intrinsic interest in lecture, recitation, laboratory or reading assignments. (The term intrinsic interest is here used to connote genuine psychological involvement, pursuit of the work as a satisfying end in itself rather than an extrinsic interest where work is merely a means to an end.) Academic work performed principally as a chore, necessary to maintain one's status as a student. Attitude toward intellectual pursuits either neutral or definitely anti-intellectual.

2. No evidence of intrinsic interest in academic work but favorable attitude toward becoming involved in one's studies. Envious of those who do like their work.

3. Genuine satisfaction in academic work but only for brief and scattered moments. (This is a beachhead category in which bases of satisfaction are held on only a very tenuous basis.)

4. A strong intrinsic interest but only for part of the studies, i.e., one or two courses or an equivalent segment of the academic load. The dividing line between a *weak*

and a *strong* interest in a course was at that point where the student either anticipated or experienced satisfaction for half of the semester participation in the work of that course.[1]

5. A strong intrinsic interest in all or most courses.

Scale II—*Satisfaction from friendship with peers*
1. Aloof in relationships with peers. Gives evidence neither of attraction to other students nor an awareness that a closer relationship can yield satisfaction.
2. Actively seeks closer interpersonal relationships with peers yet seems unsuccessful in this endeavor.
3. Enjoys moderal attachments to one or more other students. Occasionally experiences the satisfaction gained in a close friendship.[2] Yet has difficulty in re-establishing such a relationship with the same party again.
4. Enjoys a close friendship with one or more peers but such friendships seem to exist within a restricted social sphere. Either shows no interest in forming new friendships beyond his group or experiences great difficulty when such an attempt is made.
5. Forms and maintains a close friendship with other students with varying temperament and social background. Such friendships may not number more than

---

1. Such a distinction between levels of satisfaction places relatively greater emphasis on temporal maintenance of an interest, seemingly giving no weight to occasional but deep experiences. It is for this reason that consideration was also given to anticipation of satisfaction.

2. Close friendship is a term here used to connote a particular kind of interpersonal relationship. It is variously described as a meeting of minds, sharing of inner-selves, or sharing of ideas of high personal significance to each party. A positive regard or feeling for each other must exist but the relationship must be collateral to the extent that one party is not emotionally dependent on the other. The relationship is liberating and not restrictive in nature. Each party must feel free to establish and maintain other close friendships.

three or four. Emphasis remains on quality and not quantity of friendships.

(A few words are in order concerning how differential judgments were made in utilizing these first two rating scales. Information gained from the student himself formed the primary basis for making the ratings. Occasionally this was supplemented by our observations of the student in a more social context. The students, of course, were unaware of the existence of this rating scheme. In fact, I had to be careful not to betray the fact that such judgments were being made.)

Scale III—*Self-understanding and acceptance*

1. Profoundly naïve about oneself. Seems to avoid self-inspection altogether; or tortures oneself almost obsessively about imagined deficiencies of the self.

2. Same as above except for experiencing periods when there appears to be some realistic facing up to one's real difficulties. These attempts, however, seem to be unsuccessful with the consequence of a return to a state of naïve unconcern; or to a state of genuine despair.

3. A moderate dislike of most aspects of the self but has been able to establish a beachhead, a basis for a more hopeful fulfillment without dependence upon others for encouragement.

4. Acceptance of most aspects of the self including the deeper impulses but maintains realistic reservations about certain aspects of the self which on occasion cause serious concern. Demonstrates a moderate degree of self-objectivity.

5. Enjoys one's own company. Is able to see the personal dilemmas, as they arise, in an objective and sometimes humorous light. Takes satisfaction in attacking personal problems constructively.

Once the limits of the impulse-control dimension were

defined in terms of the three prototypes and their respective position on the arc aspect of the model, a student's position on this dimension could be judged. The lower a person is on the developmental dimension the easier, of course, is the judgment on the temperamental dimension. As the student develops toward the ego functioning of the Reasonable Adventurer, the less he exhibits the characteristics of X, Y, or Z or intervening points on the arc. The high X exhibits more spark and liveliness, the high Y more warmth, and the high Z greater control than their lower counterparts.

While the transcripts of over 700 interviews served as the primary bases of analysis for making judgments on both dimensions, the writer had many opportunities to observe the project members in settings beyond the interview. For example, the project was divided into four discussion groups of nine men each. Each group met several times a semester in the evening, sometimes for four or five hours if an interesting session developed. The composition of the discussion groups was altered each semester. Many a time a new aspect of an individual would come into view, one not apparent in the interview. In general, however, impressions gained in one setting simply reinforced that received in another. To the interviews and discussion group must be added the more impromptu meetings on the campus and visits to one's home as well as opportunities to observe the various project members while they were participating in athletics and other extracurricular events.

Formal testing was used sparsely and then only toward the end of the four-year project. At that time there was a natural interest in a variety of techniques that might lead toward quantification of some of the variables used in the personality framework of this study. My relationship with the project members was that of faculty adviser and friend. The students were most generous with their time. It was given without thought of compensation. To those gracious enough to include me as a participant observer in their life, the shift to another role would have seemed strange if not improper. Hopefully, subjective studies such as the one reported in this essay may do much to lay the groundwork for experimental studies in the future.